THE TEXAS LIBERATORS

THE TEXAS LIBERATORS

VETERAN NARRATIVES FROM WORLD WAR II

Edited by Aliza S. Wong | Foreword by Ron Milam
Photographs by Mark Umstot

Texas Tech University Press

This book is typeset in Scala. The paper used in this book meets the minimum requirements of ANSI/NISO Z39.48-1992 (R1997). ∞

Designed by Kasey McBeath
Cover photograph by Mark Umstot

Library of Congress Cataloging-in-Publication Data
Names: Wong, Aliza S., editor.
Title: The Texas liberators : veteran narratives from World War II / edited by Aliza S. Wong.
Description: Lubbock, Texas : Texas Tech University Press, 2017. | Includes index.
Identifiers: LCCN 2017028344| ISBN 9781682830239 (hardcover-vip : alk. paper) | ISBN 9781682830246 (hardcover : alk. paper) | ISBN 9781682830253 (pbk. : alk. paper)

Subjects: LCSH: World War, 1939-1945—Veterans—Texas—Interviews. | World War, 1939-1945—Veterans—Texas—Biography. | World War, 1939-1945—Personal narratives, American. | Holocaust, Jewish (1939-1945—Personal narratives. | United States—Armed Forces—Biography.
Classification: LCC D810.V42 U684 2017 | DDC 940.54/810922 [B]—dc23 LC record available at https://lccn.loc.gov/2017028344

18 19 20 21 22 23 24 25 26 / 9 8 7 6 5 4 3 2 1

Texas Tech University Press
Box 41037 | Lubbock, Texas 79409-1037 USA
800.832.4042 | ttup@ttu.edu | www.ttupress.org

To all those who have suffered human indignity,

to all those who have survived human indecency,

to all those who lived the Holocaust,

and to all those who found the courage to seek liberation.

In memory of the victims and survivors of one of the darkest chapters of human history and in gratitude to the liberators who sought to defend human dignity.

CONTENTS

FOREWORD
American Liberators in the Second World War

World War II has been described by most historians as the largest and bloodiest event in human history.[1] While exact numbers of those killed range from fifty million to sixty million, with millions more wounded physically or mentally, the numbers are but part of the story. As in World War I, the United States watched the world at war from afar and tried to avoid entry. As a result of the controversy surrounding the end of World War I and the Treaty of Versailles, isolationist attitudes prevailed and politicians ran on platforms of not sending American boys to fight in Europe. Through the Lend-Lease program, the United States helped the British fight the Nazi regime by lending and repairing ships to allow material to reach the British Isles through the German blockades. Yet even this was too much involvement for much of the American public. Newspapers such as the *Chicago Tribune* published editorial cartoons critical of President Franklin D. Roosevelt's apparent desire to become more involved in the war.[2] So Americans watched and some supported Adolf Hitler as Germany stormed its way across Europe.

On December 7, 1941, "a day that will live in infamy," Japan attacked United States naval forces at Pearl Harbor, Hawaii.[3] The US Congress declared war on Japan the next day and three days later Germany declared war on the United States. Thus, the nation that had successfully negotiated or conquered its way through most of Europe and the Soviet Union now had to confront a new belligerent—one with industrial and military might.

The United States was not prepared to go to war. Training camps had to be set up, factories had to convert from automobile production to tank and airplane production, and a "war footing" had to be established in both the government and society. And with the United States having been attacked by the Empire of Japan, many citizens were more concerned about revenge than about the war in Europe. President Roosevelt and his military commanders were confronted with a multiple-front war that would require many soldiers, sailors, pilots, and marines, along with support civilians. Women, more so than ever before, would also be called on to take factory jobs to produce war material and, as the war went on, to take on roles overseas as nurses, pilots, and in the armed services in Europe and the Pacific theater of operations. Unlike in World War I, the United States would launch a plan of "total war" against the Axis of Japan, Germany, and Italy and commit its entire population to the effort both home and abroad.

A draft program had been initiated in October 1940, requiring men between the ages of eighteen and sixty-five to register and to serve twelve months. These draftees were all extended, but because of the war footing, the twelve-month rule changed to "duration of the war" and more than ten million men were inducted.⁴ Many of these men would become the liberators of Europe and the liberators of those confined to Nazi prisons, concentration camps, and death camps.

Because Germany and Adolf Hitler's Nazi regime were fighting a different war within the continent, a war against the Jews, Germany would commit nearly as many resources to the eradication of Jews from Europe as it would to fighting the Allies. The consequences of this war would eventually be known as the Holocaust. Between 1933 and 1945, Nazi Germany and its allies built more than forty thousand camps and prisons. With the Wannsee Conference in 1942, when Nazi officers and senior German government officials were brought together to ensure collaboration in the implementation of the Final Solution, the scope of the plan to deport and exterminate the Jewish population in Europe required the coordination of the Reich Main Security Office, the Transport Ministry, the Main Office of the Order Police, and the Foreign Office. Some historians estimate that approximately two hundred thousand railway workers were involved in the transportation of 3 million Jews to the concentration camps.

Hitler's official rise to power began in 1933, although he had been organizing the German Worker's Party since shortly after his service in World War I. In *Mein Kampf*, written during his imprisonment for having attempted a coup in Munich, he outlined his determination to rid the world of Jews: "The nationalization of our masses will succeed only when, aside from all the positive struggle for the soul of our people, their international prisoners are exterminated."⁵ In November 1938, Jewish homes, businesses, and synagogues were destroyed in a wave of anti-Semitic aggression. *Kristallnacht*—"night of broken glass"—referred to the shattered glass that blanketed the streets in Germany, Austria, and the Sudetenland as violence erupted against the Jewish communities. The event is often considered the symbolic beginning of Hitler's Germany. With the construction of concentration, labor, and ultimately death camps, Hitler began his attempt to fulfill what he said he would do: exterminate the Jews.

Historians debate the extent to which US leaders knew about Germany's plans to eradicate the Jewish population of Europe. However, as early as July 1942, *The New York Times* reported on Chelmno and its operations as an extermination center, and in August of that year, Gerhart Riegner, representative of the

World Jewish Congress, sent a report to the State Department arguing that Nazi Germany planned to eliminate the European Jews. This missive never arrived to its intended recipient, Rabbi Stephen Wise, the president of the World Jewish Congress. The irony is that Germany continued its actions until the end of the war. Despite these warnings, laws were not changed appreciably to allow those seeking safety to enter the United States. Soldiers and marines of the United States and Allied forces were probably not fully aware of what they would find when they arrived at the camps in 1945.

The term *liberator* has a variety of meanings and applications. More than likely, those who came to be called liberators never anticipated playing that role. Very few of the soldiers and marines who would face German and Italian troops in Europe had seen combat before the war, and they would be tested in ways they could never have imagined. However, as early as 1943 all of Germany was being bombarded by radio stating that the perpetrators of crimes against humanity would be prosecuted after the war. The irony is that Germany continued their actions until the end of the war. With most US forces not arriving in Europe until the summer months of 1943 (Sicily) and the invasion of the mainland in September (Italy), Americans were more accustomed to seeing stories about the Pacific theater than watching newsreels about what was happening in Europe. But American men were being drafted to train for the largest amphibious assault in history at the coastal province of Normandy, France. Having been transported to England by boat in freezing temperatures and frightening high seas, these men trained for several months for the invasion of Europe. In Operation Overlord on D-Day they would join thousands of British and Canadian troops and jump from aircraft, assault beaches from landing craft, and kill or be killed by Germans who resisted the invasion at beaches named Utah, Omaha, Gold, Juno, and Sword.⁶ All of these men could be called liberators, for they would not only take part in the greatest military operation in history, but also continue to fight and gain terrain for ten months until they had destroyed the German army's will to fight. The allied mission was to take Berlin and to destroy the German military machine.

Thus, an American soldier who survived the beaches at Normandy would have to continue to fight until the war was over or until he was killed or wounded. This would require him to traverse the "bocage," or hedgerow, of Normandy, France, the rivers, hillsides, and pastures of Germany, and to fight in other countries of Europe, such as Belgium and Luxembourg. In operations such as Market Garden, Pegasus, and the German Operation *Wacht am Rhein,* translated as "Watch on the Rhine" and nicknamed Battle of the Bulge by reporters, Americans and their British and Canadian allies would work their way toward Berlin. In December 1945, units such as the Seventh, Tenth, and Eleventh Armored Divisions, the Thirtieth, Seventy-Fifth, and 106th Infantry Divisions, and the Eighty-Second and 101st Airborne Divisions, more than seven hundred thousand men would take part in a month long battle that would resist "the Bulge" of the German army and set up the destruction of Hitler's Nazi regime.[7]

By April 1945, Allied troops of both the United States and the Soviet Union had sufficiently established control over Germany and German-occupied Poland. After troops witnessed the horrors of a concentration camp, General Dwight D. Eisenhower ordered the forces to "liberate" the camps that had been used to imprison, force labor at gunpoint, and persecute and mass murder Jews, Roma and Sinti (Gypsies), homosexuals, communists, political prisoners, or "common" criminals. Some of these camps were the death camp at Auschwitz, Poland, liberated by Soviet soldiers on January 27, 1945; Buchenwald, a concentration camp liberated by Americans on April 11, 1945; Bergen-Belsen, a concentration camp liberated by the British on April 15, 1945; Dora-Mittelbau, a concentration camp liberated by Americans on April 11, 1945; Landsberg, one of eleven subcamps of Dachau liberated by the Texas Twelfth Armored Division on April 27, 1945; Dachau, which was the original concentration camp and was liberated by Americans on April 29, 1945; and Mauthausen, liberated by the Americans on May 5, 1945. Other camps were liberated as Allied troops discovered their existence.[8] What is most alarming and evidence of the genocide perpetuated by the Nazis was that more than 3,000,000 Jews and hundreds of thousands of others were murdered in those camps.

The liberating soldiers were shocked beyond imagination at the horrific sights they discovered in the camps. Depending on the extent and degree of malnutrition, some prisoners would attempt to hug, thank, or embrace the soldiers, but most just wept.

The memories of those moments would stay with the liberators forever.

In this compilation of interviews edited by Aliza Wong, the liberators share those memories with us. We thank them for their service.

Dr. Ron Milam
Associate Professor, Department of History
Texas Tech University

Notes

1. Although many historians have made this claim, those who have attracted the most attention and whose works were consulted for this chapter are British historian John Keegan in *The Second World War* (New York: Penguin Books, 1989), and US historian Mark Stoler in *Major Problems in the History of World War II: Documents and Essays* (New York: Houghton Mifflin Company, 2003).

2. A cartoon in the *Chicago Tribune,* November 29, 1940, was captioned, "It's Hard For Us to Understand Their Senseless Warfare, but Maybe They Have a Good Reason," and depicted a European leader pounding himself on the head with a hammer as Uncle Sam looked on. R. D. Milam's personal archives and digital archives at http://www.lib.niu.edu/2002/iht920205.html.

3. President Franklin D. Roosevelt Address to Joint Session of Congress, December 8, 1941, in *The United States in World War II: A Documentary Reader,* ed. Kurt Piehler, 55 (Malden, MA: Wiley-Blackwell, 2013).

4. George Q. Flynn, *The Draft, 1940–1973* (Lawrence: University Press of Kansas, 1993).

5. Adolf Hitler, *Mein Kampf: My Struggle,* ed. Rudolf Hess (London: Tower Books, Haole Library, 2015).

6. Alexander Swanston and Malcolm Swanston, *The Historical Atlas of World War II: 170 Maps Chart the Most Cataclysmic Event in Human History* (New York: Chartwell Books, 2010), 269.

7. Charles B. MacDonald, *A Time for Trumpets: The Untold Story of the Battle of the Bulge* (New York: Perennial, 2002).

8. Detailed information on the dates and units involved in the liberation of the Nazi camps can be found in the *Holocaust Encyclopedia* of the United States Holocaust Memorial Museum, available at https://www.ushmm.org/wlc/en/article.php?ModuleId=10005131.

March 2017

The Texas Holocaust and Genocide Commission, founded in 2009, has played a key role in the education of our students, eradication of their ignorance, and emancipation of their spirit on the issues of holocaust and genocide. It was instrumental in having the Texas Legislature declare April as Genocide Awareness and Prevention Month from 2011 to 2020.

Its Texas Veteran Liberators Project is another milestone of the Commission's great work. The Project's important components of Digital Application, Honor Roll, Book, and Traveling Exhibit will celebrate the Texas Liberators for their extraordinary courage and the uncommon sacrifice of our Greatest Generation. I salute them for their Duty to Honor our Country. May God bless them and our United States of America!

A NOTE ON THE TEXAS VETERAN LIBERATORS HONOR ROLL FROM P. N. BERKOWITZ

Former Chairman, Texas Holocaust and Genocide Commission

Before the end of the Second World War, the European liberation operations of April and May 1945 exposed the horrors committed by Nazi Germany: its deliberate dehumanization and destruction of populations—mostly Jews, Roma (Gypsies), and others whose lives were deemed worthless. The testimonies of the survivors and the gut-wrenching depictions by US Army liberators revealed unimaginable acts of previously concealed Nazi savagery. The liberation ended the sadistic treatment, including physical and psychological torture, of the prisoners.

Texas veteran liberators—those soldiers who served in one of five Texas military units—were a part of the liberation of more than forty death camps, slave labor camps, sub-camps, work camps, and POW camps. Many of these veterans documented the consequences of the Holocaust perpetrated by the Nazis and their accomplices. The stories they have told of that dark experience are the testimonies of wounded souls who witnessed such horrors. The pain suffered by the victims became their pain. Their lives were forever changed by seeing such inhumanity. The scenes they witnessed are beyond description, almost impossible to absorb. Many of those heroic veterans could not speak of those scenes for thirty, forty, or fifty years afterward. Yet, the content of their testimonies cannot be lost or ignored.

For their courage Texas veteran liberators deserve our eternal gratitude. They are honored in this book with their names in the Texas Veteran Liberators Honor Roll. A Texas veteran liberator is defined as someone who was born in Texas or lived in Texas either before or after WWII. With the help of Texas Holocaust and Genocide Commission (THGC) staff and volunteers, we have been "rescuing" Texas liberators and have compiled a list of veterans who participated in the liberation of the concentration camps. The Honor Roll includes details about each liberator, such as branch of service, years of service, hometown or place of residence, camps liberated, and dates of liberation. At the time of publication, the THGC had acquired the names of more than three hundred Texas veteran liberators who participated in forty-three different camp liberations, as members of the following Texas units, cited as official liberators of camps and subcamps:

Thirty-Sixth Infantry Division
Forty-Second Infantry Division (Oklahoma and Texas)
Forty-Fifth Infantry Division
103rd Infantry Division
Twelfth Armored Division
152nd Armed Signal Company
134th Harvester Battalion

The names thus acquired, along with expected additional names of veterans, will be cataloged into a Texas Veteran Liberators Honor Roll database available through the THGC's website and will be included in an interactive part of planned traveling exhibits.

Many more Texas veteran liberators are yet to be identified, and we welcome their inclusion in the Honor Roll. This Honor Roll is a reminder of what those veterans did for the protection of others' human rights.

The emphasis of this effort is on acknowledging the horrors suffered by the survivors and honoring those veterans who witnessed the aftermath of their traumatic experience. The words of General Dwight Eisenhower after viewing the human destruction at Ohrdruf summarize his moral indignation and give voice to American ideas of human responsibility:

> The most interesting—although horrible—sight that I encountered during the trip was a visit to a German internment camp near Gotha. The things I saw beggar description. . . . The visual evidence and the verbal testimony of starvation, cruelty and bestiality were so overpowering as to leave me a bit sick. In one room . . . were piled up twenty or thirty naked men, killed by starvation. . . . I made the visit deliberately, in order to be in a position to give first-hand evidence of these things if ever, in the future, there develops a tendency to charge these allegations merely to "propaganda."

Eisenhower's righteous indignation empowered him to insist that the world know what happened in the Nazi and death concentration camps. Eisenhower requested General George Marshall to bring members of Congress and journalists to the liberated camps. He wanted them to understand and tell the American public the horrible truth about Nazi atrocities.

We educate about the past with hope that future generations will not repeat the human failures that occurred in WWII.

THE TEXAS HOLOCAUST AND GENOCIDE COMMISSION
Texas Liberator Project

Through the combined efforts of the Texas Holocaust and Genocide Commission (THGC), editor Aliza Wong, and Texas Tech University Press, *The Texas Liberators: Veteran Narratives from World War II* fulfills in part the THGC's mission to "promote awareness of the Holocaust and genocides, to educate and inspire our citizens in the prevention of future atrocities."

Among the THGC's goals is to educate teachers and students to better understand the consequences of hatred, bigotry, and apathy. This focus on student education is an investment in our future. The THGC was established with Texas Senate Bill (SB) 482. The bill, which was initiated and backed by Holocaust Museum Houston, was passed unanimously by both the Texas House of Representatives and the Texas Senate and was signed into law by then-Governor Rick Perry on June 19, 2009. SB 482 was introduced by Senators Rodney Ellis (Houston) and Florence Shapiro (Plano) during the Eighty-First Texas Legislative Session. House Bill 795, the identical partner to SB 482, was authored primarily by Texas State Representatives Warren Chisum (Pampa) and Ellen Cohen (Houston).

The purpose of SB 482 was to help ensure that educators in Texas have the guidance and resources necessary to teach children the lessons of the Holocaust and other contemporary genocides. To meet this mandate, the THGC provides advice and assistance to public and private primary schools, secondary schools, and institutions of higher education regarding implementation of Holocaust and genocide courses of study and awareness programs. The THGC is charged with compiling a list of volunteers such as survivors of the Holocaust or other genocides, liberators of concentration camps, scholars, and members of the clergy who have agreed to share verifiable knowledge and experience regarding the Holocaust or other genocides.

The THGC is composed of fifteen commissioners, a Senate and House advisor, plus the chair of the Texas Education Agency, the chair of the Texas Board of Higher Education, and the executive director of the Texas Veterans Commission serving as ex-officio members. The Friends of THGC (Friends) was organized in 2010 as a 501(c)3 nonprofit for the purpose of supporting the programs and activities of the THGC. Since its inception the Friends have supplied funds annually for THGC programs. Several statewide programs initiated by the THGC were originally funded by the Friends, which continues to support educational programs coordinated by the THGC that benefit the citizens of Texas.

Early in 2010, the THGC went before the Texas Board of Education and asked that the Holocaust and other genocides be included in the Texas Essential Knowledge and Skills social studies curricula. Several areas of US History, World History, and World Geography were revised to include those topics. In addition to the Holocaust and other genocides, inclusion of the liberation period of World War II in student education was of critical importance to the THGC. Later in 2010, the THGC and Friends contracted to have educator workshops in all twenty Texas Education Service Regions to instruct educators on how to teach the Holocaust and other genocides. These workshops continue with THGC staff as the principal instructors.

The THGC initiated a project in 2012 to collect the oral history testimonies of Texas veterans of World War II who were not previously interviewed by Texas Holocaust museums or the Shoah Foundation, to provide Texas educators with additional resources on the liberation period. The THGC contracted with Baylor University's Institute for Oral History to record and preserve nineteen Texas veteran liberator oral history video testimonies. These testimonies are available on the THGC website.

In 2014, the THGC attended a US Holocaust Museum Southwest area discussion held in Dallas, where commissioners inquired why Advance Placement (AP) students did not study the Holocaust in their US History, European History, and World History curricula. The response was that the AP curricula are developed by the College Board for all US, Canada, and worldwide schools using the AP programs. With this information, the THGC began discussions with the College Board in New York to ask that the Holocaust and other genocides be included in their history curricula. In 2015, the College Board agreed to include the Holocaust and other genocides in their European and World History curricula. Continued work with the College Board resulted in the inclusion of the liberation period of World War II in their US History curriculum in 2016.

This major accomplishment, along with the State of Texas requirement to teach the liberation period in schools, resulted in the THGC's responsibility to prepare accessible classroom material for educating students. To meet this opportunity, the THGC requested proposals from Texas universities for an approach to teaching this topic. In 2015, Texas Tech University was selected to prepare the material based on its proposal to develop an interactive app, classroom material, and a book that met the following

core educational goals and learning outcomes (in line with TEKS and the AP exam):

- Students will understand the context of the Second World War and be able to place the Holocaust within that historical framework.
- Students will engage with composite historical actors and will grasp the significance of
    - the profundity of calculated, systematic genocide during World War II
    - the role of the death camps in the "Final Solution"
    - the significance of US soldiers' experiences as they came upon work and death camps in Europe
    - the role of the US military in the final stages of the war
    - the role of the US military in the liberation of the camps
    - the psychological and emotional effects of witnessing these atrocities on US soldiers
    - the importance of remembering the Holocaust, its survivors and victims, and of honoring the US liberators
- Students will be exposed to historical work, the use of primary documents, texts, oral interviews, videos, artifacts, and other materials, and the ways in which they tell a narrative about the human past and condition.
- Students will be able to think critically, to analyze evidence, and to communicate the historical narrative of the liberation, the Holocaust, its context, and its legacy.
- Students will be able to evaluate the different texts of the digital app—testimonial, letters, objects, artwork, and literature.
- Students will be able to explain the complexities of war, the duties and responsibilities of soldiers, and the consequences of war on all populations.

With the publication of *The Texas Liberators: Veteran Narratives from World War II,* the THGC is providing one book to each of the 3,709 public and private high schools in Texas. This book, the mobile application, and the THGC website will benefit over

11,160 schools serving 5,309,430 students by 344,879 teachers, greatly benefitting the State of Texas.

Since every high school will have access to the lesson plans via the THGC and Texas Tech University websites, Texas students and more than 515,000 AP students nationwide are expected to be exposed to this content within the next two years.

ACKNOWLEDGMENTS

In 2009, then Texas state senator Florence Shapiro's hope for the future of Texans helped lead to the creation of the commission. Along with Senator Rodney Ellis, Shapiro introduced SB 482. Texas State Representatives Warren Chisum and Ellen Cohen were the primary authors of HB 795, the partner to SB 482. Private citizens, such as Susan Myers, added their voices to those of the legislature. Governor Rick Perry signed the Senate bill into law. Without these inspiring efforts to create the THGC, the concept of honoring Texas liberators would not have become a reality.

Educational materials on the THGC website were made possible through guidance and support from Texas institutions, organizations, and individuals throughout the United States.

THGC's journey to bring an understanding of the consequences of genocide to all Texas students began in 2010 with the Texas State Board of Education, whose members adapted TEKS for social studies to include the Holocaust and modern genocides. Commissioners felt that the best vehicle for teaching students about Nazi concentration, slave labor, and death camps was testimony from the Texas veterans who liberated those camps. With insightful guidance from Stephen M. Sloan, Baylor University's Institute for Oral History (IFOH) video recorded the testimonies of nineteen Texas veteran liberators who had not previously been interviewed by the Texas Holocaust museums. These videos and transcripts were completed by Robert DeBoard, Megan Genovese, Courtney Lyons, Elinor Maze, and Sloan. These testimonies were posted on THGC's website and are in the US Library of Congress' Veterans History Project. With help from archivist Carol Manley at Holocaust Museum Houston, THGC digitized twenty-seven additional video interviews. The Dallas Holocaust Museum provided another twenty Liberator names, and the El Paso Holocaust Museum provided Liberator names who were stationed at Fort Bliss at the end of WWII. In each case, staff and volunteers worked countless hours preserving and transcribing as possible, and their actions significantly aided this project.

In 2015, College Board coordinators Lawrence Charap and Allison Thurber were instrumental in including World War II Liberation in the 2016 AP American, European, and World History curricula. Providing resources for these topics, TTU received a contract from THGC for the Texas Liberator Project. Aliza S. Wong, TTU Honors College, managed the enormous task of bringing the program to fruition. Her team included Jiawei Gong, J.T. and Margaret Talkington College of Visual And Performing Arts; Robert Peaslee and Randy Reddick, College of

Media and Communication; and Christian Pongratz, formerly of the College of Architecture. The Project was designed, scripted, and programmed by TTU professors and undergraduate and graduate students in the TTU Honors College, College of Media and Communication, and the College of Arts and Sciences.

THGC thanks Courtney Burkholder and Amanda Werts, Texas Tech University Press, and Monty Monroe, PhD, Museum of Texas Tech University, for their contributions to the program. A special thank you to Texas Tech administrators, Senior Vice Provost Rob Stewart, Provost Michael Galyean, and President Lawrence Schovanec for their support of this innovative approach to academic teaching.

The names for the Texas Veteran Liberator Honor Roll was made possible with research and assistance from:

Gregg Bailey and Anton DuPlessis, Texas A&M Cushing Memorial Library

Mike Becket, 45th Infantry Division Museum

Daughters of the American Revolution, Sam Houston Chapter

Harry Dhans, 12th Armored Division Museum

Owen Glendening, National WWII Museum

Wanda Guinn, Hutchinson County Historical Museum

Mary Pat Higgins, Dallas Holocaust Museum/Center for Education & Tolerance

Toni Nickel, Shoah Foundation, Texas A&M University

Lori Shepard and Jamie Williams, El Paso Holocaust Museum and Study Center

Janice Adamson Splawn and Kelly J. Zúñiga, Holocaust Museum Houston

United States Holocaust Memorial Museum

VOCES Project, University of Texas

Larry Wayne, 103rd Infantry Division WWII Association

Mike Glenn's magnificent *Houston Chronicle* article about the Texas Veteran Liberator Honor Roll attracted names from veteran and Liberator families. Sam Malone created the www.TexasLiberators.com website and publicity releases distributed by 512 New Media. Steven Wolf coordinated transportation to the commemoration event launching the APP and the Honor Roll.

Available to students and teachers throughout the United States at no charge, the Texas Veteran Liberator Project, would not have been possible without the extraordinary commitment of the THGC staff: Cheyanne Perkins, William McWhorter, Charles Sadnick, Lynn Santos, and Jake Wolfson. Through dedication and resolve, they coordinated the many component parts that make up this project. THGC is also indebted to Commissioners Fran Berg, Frank Kasman, and Suzanne Ransleben for the foresight and leadership that made this a success.

Finally, we wish to thank Commissioner Peter N. Berkowitz, truly the architect of this project. His work to have the Texas Board of Education and the College Board's Advance Placement (AP) history curriculums include the liberation period initiated the educational programs developed to fulfill THGC's mission. His persistence in personally identifying as many Texas Liberators as possible to create the project's Honor Roll, which lists more than 300 veterans by name, has made this undertaking the success that it is.

No program of this magnitude can be accomplished without the financial support of the State of Texas, Texas Tech University, and the Friends of Texas Holocaust & Genocide Commission. The following foundations, organizations and individuals are to be acknowledged for their contributions to the Texas Liberator Project:

Stanford and Joan Alexander Foundation

Fran and Mark Berg

Charlotte and Peter Berkowitz

Dallas Holocaust Museum/Center for Education and Tolerance

El Paso Holocaust Museum and Study Center

HFW Fund & Helfman Dealerships

Albert and Ethel Herzstein Charitable Foundation

Holocaust Museum Houston

Frank Kasman

Ed Rachal Foundation

Regina Rogers

The Summerlee Foundation

INTRODUCTION

When Senior Vice Provost of Texas Tech University Dr. Rob Stewart invited me to a meeting with the Texas Holocaust and Genocide Commission (THGC), represented by Mr. Peter Berkowitz, I had no idea of the amazing, humbling, inspiring, horrifying, jaw-dropping, overwhelming, breathtaking project I was about to take on. After a series of discussions with Berkowitz and Dr. Frank Kasman, another commissioner with the THGC, several phone calls with program specialist Cheyanne Perkins, a meeting with Executive Director William McWhorter, proposals, and negotiations, the THGC and Texas Tech University (TTU) embarked on this quest together—to create an engaging, innovative, interactive educational tool that would introduce Texas high school students to the story of the Holocaust, honor the heroism of our Texas soldiers who fought in the Second World War, and continue the important work of remembering the humanity and inhumanity of the war. The computer app will be distributed to high schools in the state of Texas and will be enhanced by a website that will have numerous resources for teachers, students, and the general public who would like to learn more about Texas liberators in the Second World War and the history of the Holocaust. Perhaps most impressively, the vast majority of the work on this project, from historical research to film production, from

3D architectural rendering to graphic design, from computer programming to text and narrative, has been created by Texas Tech graduate and undergraduate students in a cross-college collaboration that truly speaks to the interdisciplinary vision of Texas Tech University.

A traveling museum exhibit features the app, the book, the website, and the history of the Second World War. With its twenty-one free-standing panels, each one honoring the Texas liberators featured in the Liberator Project, this traveling exhibit has been designed not only by museum staff and experts, but also with the input of our students who hope to move into the world of museum curating and historical preservation.

This book hopes to preserve these stories and these experiences for many generations to come. By allowing these men to speak in their own words, to reveal to us their discovery of the camps, the ways in which they remember their first encounters, the ways in which they chose to forget in order to survive, the ways in which they lived with their survival, the ways in which normal was never normal again, the ways in which they honor us with their stories now—we help to liberate the memories of these men so that everyone can understand the sacrifices made in the name of freedom. The Honor Roll included at the end of this volume is the work of Peter Berkowitz, who made it his mission these past few years to "rescue" these liberators, to find them, their names, their ranks, their narratives in order to honor them here.

After successfully working to get this part of US History added to the Texas Essential Knowledge and Skills in schools, the THGC canvassed Texas looking for Liberators to interview to provide resources for educators and students through the veterans' testimonies. Due to their age, there are truly not that many available, but the THGC found nineteen. Nineteen of the twenty-one interviews were conducted by Baylor a few years ago with the other two testimonies added later. These twenty-one testimonies made up the material the THGC brought to TTU to create the app and book. Since the first nineteen oral history interviews, over 300 liberators have been identified.

One of the most difficult tasks as an editor and as a historian is to retain the integrity of the original document while also shaping a fluid and compelling narrative. The oral histories we have included ranged from two to four hours long, with interventions by the archivist as well as interruptions by others in the household, grandfather clocks, pets, and offers of iced tea and lemonade. In an effort to maintain the integrity of the veterans' voices—their intonations, their hesitations and falterings, their asides and misrememberings, their quirks and personalities, the very intimacy of the telling, the witnessing of these stories—I decided, as the editor, to include all of the stops and starts as they happened in the interviews. I did, however, take authorial liberty with removing the voice of the interviewer, as I wanted these men to tell their own stories, to truly record their narratives as historical documents. While this approach may not lend itself to the smoothest reading, I believe firmly that these men deserve to be honored by having their stories remembered as their own stories. In their own words. In their own time. Whatever imperfections that may arise from this editorial decision are mine alone. The heroism, the humility, the humor, and the honor with which these men share their histories—that is theirs alone.

The Liberator Project, with its many layers and tiers and levels, has surprised me and shocked me and saddened me and uplifted me. I am changed because of this project. I am smaller because I have seen greatness and sacrifice and survival and freedom through the eyes of those who were victimized, those who were liberators, those who charge us, challenge us to never forget. And I am bigger because their strengths and weaknesses, their honesty and good humor, their tragedies and narratives have reminded me always that we must tell this story over and over and over again. Because as much as this is their story, the story of six million Jewish people who were killed and their families who live on without them, the story of "undesirables" who were euthanized, sterilized, experimented upon, enslaved, executed, the story of more than sixteen million American men and women who served their nation in the United States military during the Second World War, and the story of the twenty-one Texas liberators whose tales are featured here in this volume— this is also *our* story, *our* history. This is the history not only of one of the world's most devastating crimes against humanity, but also the history of some of the most incredible tales of bravery, selflessness, and heroism.

This is their story.

And may we make it indelibly our own so that we never forget.

Dr. Aliza S. Wong
Associate Dean, Honors College
Associate Professor, Department of History
Texas Tech University

THE TEXAS LIBERATORS

ROBERT P. ANDERSON

Excerpts from the interview conducted by Stephen M. Sloan

May 17, 2012

[B]oth of us have come from Swedish families. And I lived in—in my early life, I was very closely associated with a Swedish church. The denomination is the Covenant, the Evangelical Covenant. At that time it was Swedish. So my early, early years were centered on Sweden, really. I mean, you know, our—all my grandparents came from Sweden, and my parents spoke Swedish and so on. But unfortunately, they didn't speak Swedish to us.

And I lived in the South Side of Chicago and went to elementary school and high school—Calumet High School in Chicago. And when I was about eleven, my father passed away. And then, later, my mother passed away. And I lived with my sister. I didn't know anybody else but Swedes, although I lived in a— I hesitate to say it this way, but another, broader ethnic community that was Roman Catholic. And so I was actually a minority. . . . And we—I suppose this might be of some interest—we had Irish mafia bootleggers in our neighborhood, very close to us. I always like to tell the story that I remember as a kid, when I was very young, Al Capone coming down the alley with his machine gun, shooting up our neighbors. And so I never went out with my daddy and shot rabbits. We had the Chicago mafia trying to knock off the neighbors, which they were succeeding in doing to a certain extent.

. . . I'd always wanted to go to school. And since in the late— early forties and so on, there wasn't much money, when I graduated from high school, I started at Illinois Institute of Technology, which is the old Armour Engineering school. I started in a co-op program. In other words, we went to school one semester and then worked a semester, and so on. I was in that program, and I started in '42. At the time I was, like, eighteen and a half, or something like that. And while there, of course, the war was going on, and many of us enlisted in the army or air force or—all four services at that time. So I wasn't drafted. We anticipated going to school. At least, I was in the Air Corps and anticipated going to school for a degree, but in March of 1943 they called us all up. And that was it, after about a year of school.

Well, the recruiters came to the university. And they encouraged us to enlist, and everybody did. I mean, you know, if you weren't in the—weren't being drafted—I was eighteen—if you weren't drafted, why, you weren't so good. So we had a choice of, you know, coast guard or marines or navy or air force or army. You could enlist. And we did that . . . with the idea in mind that you would complete your education.

So it was March 1943, and I went through the normal routine and wound up in St. Petersburg, Florida, for basic training in the air force. And we had a real rough time. I lived in a hotel that they had taken over as a barracks, but went through all the preliminaries, you know, the marching and all that stuff. And then following that, I was assigned to training as a radar operator. And I spent time doing some instructing and so on, in radar, which was new at the time, and had quite a bit of experience around Bradenton-Sarasota, Florida, and that area. Then this business about the Army Specialized Training Program came out.

And so I applied for [the program], and I was accepted. . . . I was sent up to the University of Georgia in Athens. And this was in engineering. And the idea was that we were to go on and finish our degree programs, but as you probably know, there were some two hundred and fifty thousand young men who were in the ASTP programs all over the nation. In March of 1944, General [George] Marshall decided that the ASTP program was expendable and they needed troops to fill out the divisions that were going to Europe for the big invasion. And so they canceled the two hundred and—the programs all over the nation. And all of us were put into various divisions.

Oh, boy. We didn't know what was going to happen. I mean, they put us on a bus, and we went down to the Tenth Armored Division. And eight hundred of us went into the Tenth Armored as privates. Of course, the Tenth Armored was an established division. It formed in 1942, so it was—I mean, they had the officers and the enlisted people, and the noncommissioned officers, and so on, and we were just—we just filled in. I was fortunate. Since I had been in radar, I was put into the signal company, the 150th Signal Company. But many of my friends either went to be tankers or infantry, and so on. I probably wouldn't be here if it hadn't been that way. And so we went in March of '44 and by September, the division was sent overseas.

. . . We assumed, as an armored division, we were probably going to Europe.

What did I think? I am not a soldier. You know, I adapted. I did what I had to do. But it wasn't my thing. And you just—you just did what you had to do. There was no real love for it and so on. Although a great deal of loyalty developed. . . .

And so we finally got over to Europe, and my division was the first division to land directly in France. And we landed in Cherbourg. And Cherbourg had just—Let's see, that was in late September and so on. And of course, the invasion was in June, so they had just cleared out that whole Normandy area. So we came in at Cherbourg and did our staging—getting ready—in Normandy. So my first experience in Europe was in Normandy, with the hedgerows and so on. Living in pup tents, with a lot of rain.

I was in the signal company. I was a wire man. [I] had to climb telephone poles and lay the wire. And at that point we had two vehicles in our unit. One was a half-track and the other was a jeep. So we had those two vehicles, and they had reels of wire on them, you know. And you had the climbers and all that sort of stuff. And the telephone switchboard. . . . So that's what we were learning how to do, of course. A guy like myself hadn't been very well trained because we hadn't been with the division before. So we came in as pretty raw, pretty raw.

But we left there in either late October or early November [of 1944] and headed out across France to the "front lines," which was at that time around Metz, in Alsace-Lorraine region. So we went through Paris. My first experience in Paris was riding down the Champs-Élysées in a half-track, under the Arc de Triomphe and on the way.

. . .

[When we arrived in the Memmingen area], we just went into the camp. . . . I think it was a work camp, yeah. It was not a death camp. Well, I mean, I'm sure people died right and left, but it was a work camp. . . .

I mean, my experience—I have to talk about my experience. . . . My experience was, all of a sudden, here we are, we're in a camp. And seeing those, those barracks that they have there. And, "Don't talk to the soldiers. There's a lot of Americans here. You can see their picture. Don't talk to them." I remember that, because there might be German spies. And that was my first experience at seeing men—people with the striped uniforms that you've seen in the pictures. So that they—whether—the picture here is of American prisoners, there were really a lot of real concentration camp people.

. . . [T]he other thing that struck me was they were—they looked like Mongolians. And they must have been from Russia or something like that. But there was a lot of people that didn't look like Germans or didn't look like us Caucasians. They were obviously from a different ethnic group. And they were wearing the striped uniforms. And they were, they were milling around and so on. They didn't want us to have any contact with them. See, this was the first day that we were into this situation. You may not be familiar, or maybe you are, with how we are fed. You're fed off the back of a truck, and they have three GI cans. And you dip your—throw your garbage in one, and you dip your mess kit into another and you clean it, and then rinse it off over here. And what I remember is those guys in those uniforms standing by the garbage, eating it.

• • •

And I suppose another experience that I had in Thionville . . . a very lasting, uncomfortable memory, is that we didn't have a lot of heavy clothing. We were getting it gradually, but we had— As a wire man you had to go out and you work with your hands, so you had gloves. And I lost a glove. And there was no other glove, so I was out a glove. So we were parked on a road in the convoy. And I looked over there, and there was a whole pile of soldiers, dead soldiers. They just lined them up on the road, you know, and then they were waiting for the mortuary trucks to come and pick them up. But they were mostly German soldiers. There was one American from our division, who had been killed the night before. So I went through those [bodies], looking for gloves. I found a glove.

And—excuse me . . .

I took [the gloves] from a young German soldier, and on his belt, he had "God is with us." *Gott mit uns.* . . . [And] my thought was, "Jesus, I've been praying to God all my life." And he was my enemy, but the same thing. It didn't make sense. It didn't make any sense at all.

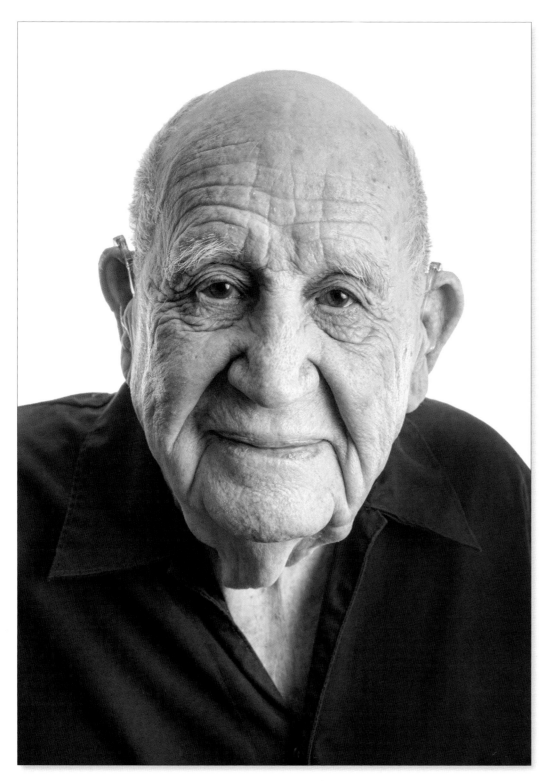

RAY BUCHANAN

Excerpts from an interview conducted by Stephen M. Sloan

November 6, 2012

In 1702, two brothers from Scotland came to the United States, in Tennessee. And we originally came from one of those Buchanans. They came down to Tennessee and raised the family there. My great-grandfather was buried in Howell, Tennessee. And, see, they had, I think it was, about five children. And my granddaddy was James Chambers Buchanan. And there— He was born in 1845 in Tennessee. And he was at home when the Civil War broke out. Well, all his brothers joined the army. And he was too young to go at that time, so he run off and joined anyhow. And his daddy went and found him and brought him back to the farm to work the farm. And he didn't like that, so he run off again. He was only fifteen years old, I think it was, at that time. He run off again and joined the cavalry again, Forrest's cavalry. All of them was in the Forrest cavalry.

So my granddaddy was at home when the Yankees had taken over Tennessee. . . . And my uncles all was older than him. And so they kind of had taken care of my granddaddy. All my uncles was wounded at least one time and lived over it. And my granddaddy was wounded in the back of his leg. And we always asked him how come he was wounded in the back of his leg, you know.

And he said, "I was just getting in a better position, you see." And that was the way he'd said it.

My daddy was born here in Mount Pleasant [Texas] in 1888. My father was married around sixty-five years and never had a death in the family. . . . And I told my daddy how lucky he was to be married sixty-five years and never have a death in the family. And he agreed that they was lucky. So we had not one death and there was seven of us, and there's still four of us still living, still living. So the doctor has told me that I have the best genes that there are, and I'll probably live a long time yet. So he may be right, I don't know.

My father was a farmer. He raised everything that you eat. We raised everything on the farm. We never went hungry, even during the Depression. He always had plenty of food on the table. And even families would come and eat with us on Sunday that didn't have anything. We wondered why we had company all the time, but it was people that didn't have nothing to eat. So my daddy would work all day. And he'd come in at noon. And he'd take that old double-barreled shotgun and go down on the banks down there. And we had mulberries, trees. The squirrels would like mulberries. And he'd kill a squirrel, bring it home, and that's what we'd have for supper is that squirrel. My mother raised a lot of chickens, so we'd have chicken on Sunday. We had plenty to eat, but a lot of families did not have a lot to eat during the Depression.

I was in high school when they hit Pearl Harbor. I knew I was going to go to war, here now. So we got married. And I stayed out a little while before they drafted me in '43. [When I] got to Camp Wolters, they'd run us through all kinds of tests, see what they wanted in the army. See what we could use—the signal corps and all that. But anyhow, we found out that the paratroopers paid fifty dollars a month more. Not thinking about the reason they're paying it, because you don't live long jumping out of a plane, you know, into combat.

They sent us to Camp Toccoa, Georgia, with the Seventeenth Parachute Infantry. And they were already in training. And we had to go through all that jumping out of the tower, doing push-ups. . . . [Eventually], we came back to Camp Hulen, Texas, down here at the antiaircraft, 838. Then they had about two hundred of us that come in there together. And so then they shipped about six hundred to eight hundred Yankees from New York and around up there, mixed with us. We was all Southern. That's when the Civil War ended, you know. During World War II, they mixed the Southern boys with the Yankees, you see. That did away with the Civil War.

So they give us all a ten-day leave. So I come home. I told my wife, I says, "When I go back, if you don't hear from me for a while, you know I got on a boat and I'm going overseas. Because I think we're going to leave as soon as we all get back." And sure enough, when we got back they loaded us all up, went to New York, and loaded us on the boat on December 1, 1944, I guess it was. Well, we was on a convoy. On clear days, you could see—count at least fifty ships in that convoy. We were in the middle, and they had all these destroyers and sub chasers around us, you see, protecting us. And it'd taken us thirteen days at sea, and we landed on a northern part of England. And we got off the boat there and loaded on a train in England. And we went all the way across England to the southern part of England, to a little small town.

On about the twentieth of December, they called us and alerted us to get ready to ship out. Well, we didn't know what was going on. It was the Belgian Bulge. And old Patton said, "Get all

them antiaircraft units and turn them into infantry and let's get up here." So that's the reason they alerted us, you know, "Get ready." But we didn't know what was going on. We didn't know there was a Belgian Bulge, that they was having trouble. So on Christmas Day they canceled our orders. They didn't need us now. See, they done stopped them. Old Patton and all of them had done stopped them. So we didn't get to go. So we waited about ten more days and got everything ready. And we went and loaded on them big landing crafts down there at Southampton. We landed all our trucks and guns. It all hooked up. And we drove them right into the end of them boats, in line, the whole outfit. And we got on that. And at night, we went across the channel. They almost had run into another boat that night, and I fell out of my bunk. We didn't know what was going on, and we asked what was going on. Said, "Well, we almost hit another boat, see, going across there." Well, we got across the next morning, and they run this boat up to the ramp. Anyhow, we drove our trucks right on out. And we went to a camp there called Lucky Strike. And there's where they issued us our ammunition, all our ammunition and everything to fight with. And so we got all that, and then we loaded up on our trucks and everything. And we went around the southern part of Paris and joined the Seventh Army over there. We just kept driving and driving. And I kept hearing artillery shells, and we got closer and closer. After a while, they was firing back from us. We'd done passed our artillery. So we went up there—and this was three o'clock in the morning.

Now, I'm nineteen years old and my buddies are nineteen years old, in a strange country you don't know where in the hell you are. They give me a little map, and it had a fence up there and it had a patch of woods there. And I was to go up there and find that place with the woods up there, where I was going to put my gun, the 40-millimeter and the .50-caliber machine gun. So we got out, me and two more, and we ease up that fence row, scared to death. Didn't know what—where the Germans was. We didn't know nothing. Three o'clock in the morning, had a little flashlight, we was afraid to use it. Afraid, you know, Germans would see us and shell and kill us.

But I went on up there and we found the place. Then we come back. It had taken about an hour's time. We told them to follow us. So we got in our trucks and we went up there. It was the right place. We put our gun in position around there and unloaded everything. And at daybreak, when it got light, I looked down in the valley there. And I never seen so many five-gallon cans of gasoline in my life, stacked up there for half a mile. And that was what we was supposed to guard. You know, if a plane come in and drop a bomb on that gasoline, it'd just all blow up, you see? And I didn't know what we was supposed to do, but that was what we was supposed to do. If any plane tried to bomb that gasoline, well, we was supposed to shoot it down.

• • •

We got word that there was a prison camp up there, up the road there. Well, all them boys wanted to get in on it, you know, my gun section and all. They wanted to go up there and see about this prison camp. So we all went up there to see what was going on. So the infantry had already taken over the camp just a few hours before we got there.

But you know how GIs are. They want to help out. They want to get in on it. So we went up there to see. Now, I went up there, and I've never seen such a sight in my life. That was just—dead people in carloads, and all them walking around there with no flesh, just bones and—just hundreds and hundreds of them. Thousands of them. Just made me sick. I didn't want to see no more of it. And I got pictures of it in there. I didn't have a camera, myself, but my other buddies had the cameras and everything. They were taking a lot of pictures. But anyhow, I didn't want to, I didn't want to stay up there, really. The smell was awful, and to see all them people walking around there. I couldn't, I just couldn't stand it.

And the infantry we had had taken over Dachau. And it wasn't any— We didn't really have any business even being up there, because I don't think the infantry needed our help. But, you know, nineteen-year-old boys and everything, they wanted in on everything. I seen all them people and everything. And the smell of it and all them people. They said there was fifty-two carloads of dead people that went out of there that day. And they dumped them. And so I didn't stay up there very long. I was just— I went up there to see what it was all about. And that's about all I remember of that.

J. TED HARTMAN

Excerpts from an interview conducted by Stephen M. Sloan

May 17, 2012

I remember coming home from church and having the radio on and hearing the news that the Japanese had bombed Pearl Harbor. We didn't know where Pearl Harbor was. We got out the atlas and looked it up and figured out exactly where it was and what it probably meant to us. There was very much a depressed feeling throughout the nation, I think. I was—let's see—I was sixteen years of age at that time. I worked a lot, as all children in Iowa did. Most all of us had a job of some sort, and I did a lot of common labor of shoveling snow and cleaning windows and that sort of thing. I remember trying to be sure that I was earning enough money so that I could keep money in the bank if I ever needed to do something real with it and not have to do common labor the rest of my life.

. . . [In] high school, the army and the navy offered an examination for all boys. The girls, of course, at that time would not be eligible for anything like that. The examination was called the A-12—V-12 examination. If you passed grade-wise, passed that examination, the navy would send you to the college of your choice. They would give you a choice of several colleges. The army would send you for basic training first and then would send you to a college of their choice. . . . They told me that I would have possibly a year, but at least six months of college before I'd be called. So I enrolled in Iowa State. Six weeks later, I was called to active duty.

We were going to be engineers. But we were only there about two months when rumors began to surface that they were needing troops for the ground troops for the upcoming invasion. They weren't going to be allow— They weren't going to be able to just let us stay in ASTP much longer. Sure enough, at the end of ten weeks, they announced that all the ASTPs were closing except for medicine and foreign languages. They . . . sent all of us that were at the University of Oregon down to Camp Cook in California where the Eleventh Armored Division was very much in need of people. It was interesting. When we marched from the University of Oregon campus down to the train depot, the people in town lined the streets to say good-bye. We didn't realize that we had meant that much. It was very touching.

. . .

We were starting— We were leaving our camp there in England and starting across. We went in absolutely pouring down rain. The driver has to drive with his head out when you're on the road and going more than five miles an hour. There's just no way you can do it otherwise. We drove for six hours in that rain—just pouring down—to get down to the harbor at Weymouth where we were to put our tanks on these landing ship, tanks, these ships. We backed our tanks onto the ships. The prow of the ships would open up like this and then a great big door would drop down, and we backed up on that door and into the ship. We backed all our tanks on. Our tanks filled a number of ships. A number of tanks could get on one of those ships, yeah. It took several ships to take all of us.

We all loaded and then moved away from the harbor and then sat there for two days. We had the finest eating we'd had in ages. Fresh rolls and ice cream. Things we'd never heard of for months and months. It was then that the Germans had started the Battle of the Bulge, while we were starting across. We were supposed to be going to southwest France to where they had a submarine pen. . . . We were supposed to come in and block it from the land and maybe move in on it as possible. That was our assignment when we started across on the boat. Well, just as we got to France, they totally changed that. Told us we were to engage in a forced march across northern France. . . . They had us load up with all the ammunition we could take because they were having trouble getting supplies across, too. As they moved inland, they needed more trucks and—that could carry supplies on roads. So they had us load every tank with every piece of ammunition and food and supplies that we could possibly take in the tank. And then we set out on these about a five-day forced march across northern France and ended up just barely into Belgium and not far from Bastogne. That's then when we started into the Battle of the Bulge.

We spent the night just at the edge of—southwest of Bastogne, just a little—thirty miles—just at the edge of where the enemy was. Then the following morning we were to take off. Usually the artillery shoots a lot and prepares the way for us to come in. But they had not been able to get there. Our reconnaissance also had not been able to get there, so we didn't know what we were meeting. But they sent us out into the battlefield, and I kept thinking, Well, I hope all of the stuff that we've learned to do by rote we'll do by rote and it'll work. And it actually did. I had to keep low in the driver's seat. I had to keep my lid down. So I

had to look at where we were going through the periscope. And the tank commander is supposed to keep giving instructions to the driver, but he was really so occupied that he wasn't giving me very much in the way of instructions. We were doing okay. Everywhere I looked, it seemed like our tanks were going in a different direction.

That first day, we ended up gaining about five miles, which was the most that had been gained that day in the Battle of the Bulge. The first day, though, our company commander's tank was hit and he was killed. Some of his tank crew were killed and two of them were captured. Another tank with some of my best friends in it was hit. That tank commander was injured badly. His knees—legs were shot off. The Germans captured them, and they forced them to carry the tank commander up about two miles to their headquarters. This all happened the first day. The next day, we went on toward another—maybe four miles forward—a little town named Chenogne, and we fought with the infantry. Our tanks and infantry fought together very well. We spent that night outside Chenogne. Then the following day, we went into the town in force and took it with the infantry and us working together. Finally, it was clear enough for the air force to come in. Eighteen out of twenty-one houses in that town were destroyed during the battle.

• • •

Well, we were coming along—we were moving along, and this was after we had started moving more quickly, gaining more ground. All of a sudden, these people started showing up in strange-looking clothes, and we couldn't figure out what they were because we'd never seen anybody that had been in a concentration camp at that point. They started showing up in these stripes, broad stripes. No one had ever told us—I'm not sure anybody knew to tell us—about the concentration camps. We started seeing these people coming out from the trees, from the woods, and then getting in the road and getting in the way. We couldn't run over them. That's not American. They just kept—more and more and more intensely coming. We'd find some of them lying in the ditches along the road. Gradually, we began to appreciate that this was some sort of prisoner, maybe because they were wearing similar clothes. And then, over the radio they told us that they had just found out that these prisoners had been released from a concentration camp. . . . It was Buchenwald.

. . . [T]hey had been released to get in our way and to slow our path, slow us down. They did slow us down, but they would absolutely stop us and kiss the front of a tank, or they'd salute us. It was—I couldn't help but cry myself. I had never seen anything like that. I couldn't understand. Of course, I didn't know the whole background picture either, I just couldn't figure out. Some of them had their buddies with them. One of them was taking care of his buddy over on the side of the road. He wouldn't leave his buddy who, I gathered, was dying. It was just all sorts of little scenes, many scenes along the way. They kept coming, but gradually, we seemed to be able to get them to stay out of the way, and we were able to move on more. I think our infantry troops were better at dealing with them than we were because they were on the ground and could help them understand that they needed to stay away from the road so we could keep our force moving on forward.

The first dead people I saw really were kind of hard to accept. How could people do that to people? . . . I hadn't seen anything like this, and it was so different.

It was about three weeks after that, I think [that we went to Mauthausen]. . . . [O]ne of my friends was a medic. The way I got to go there was, he was going over. He was on duty of certain duty hours. He asked if I would like to go over and see this because it was so different. I said yes, I would like to see it. So he arranged for me to go over when he was going over for his duty hours. We went over, and he told me, he prepared me for it as we were going. He told me that he was—when he got there—he said he wouldn't be able to spend a lot of time because he would be very busy doing the medical things for these people that were urgent. When we got there, there were these stacks of people like cordwood. There were still fires going. It was quite eerie, and there were still fires going in the furnaces with the bones in the furnace.

Then, in the barracks where they had their people, there was so many to one bed. I can't even remember how many. You almost couldn't count them. They were all so—they were just skin and bone, every one of them. People wandering around. You

wondered how they could even move. They were just nothing but skin and bone. I was out in the grounds around there. There was a large ground around there because there was a big limestone quarry, and all around there were these skin-and-bone people wandering around kind of listlessly doing nothing, just moving around. I was glad I got to see it, but I was glad that I didn't have to stay out there.

• • •

The two times we've been back—you know, they meet every year in celebration and to thank the Eleventh Armored. There are almost twenty thousand people [who] come to that celebration. We've been there two times. I didn't know—I didn't understand that one. The first meeting we went to, we got there and, as far as you could see, there were buses from all over Europe. People come who've had a connection. Some of them were the prisoners themselves who wear a scarf made out of material from their original outfit, striped, and others were from families who had a connection. But they all had a connection from Spain, Italy, all over the place.

It's been very touching every time I went. I really got very touched about all of it. You see that and you think, "They're not going to let this happen again."

BIRNEY T. "CHICK" HAVEY

Excerpts from an interview conducted by Stephen M. Sloan

May 30, 2012

[I decided to enlist in 1942.] . . . I wanted to be a pilot, and we enlisted on the air force reserve. They were taking a long time to go to pilot school. So every Saturday morning we'd go down to the recruiting office down at the [Robert A. Young] Federal Building in downtown St. Louis and see in what position we were, if any. Finally, one sergeant got a hold of me, said, "Well, why don't you join the army unassigned. Then you'll be assigned to the air force, and you'll get to go to pilot's training school." So I took his advice and signed up. The next thing, my butt was on a train going to the mule packs in Colorado Springs, Colorado.

I kind of got a kick out of the tests that the army gave you. I guess I was more mechanically inclined. I had a fellow sitting next to me, and he copied off of my mechanical test. The joke was that after we ended up, he ended up head of the division motor pool, and he didn't know anything about mechanics. You know, he had copied off of me (*laughs*), so. And I ended up at division, too, as a statistician.

[We didn't know if we were going to North Africa or if we were going to Europe.] Not till a certain point, till we got on the trains. We headed for New York and that gave us a little hint. We rode on Pullman trains . . . to the camp in New York. We were assigned a barracks. And we got passes to visit New York City, and I got to go into New York City. [We] just hopped on a train and went there, then went down to Times Square and looked around, had a few drinks. We just kind of enjoyed it. Finally, went back home a little dizzy.

[I think I shipped out in November of '44.] We went over in a rather large troop ship. It was a captured German ship from the First World War. I was, I don't want to say comfortable, but we all had bunks, some bunks down in the holds. It was crowded, but we kind of enjoyed it. I didn't get too sick, and we just enjoyed the ocean. We went through close to South America because we went south in the Gulf Stream for quite a while. And the trip was pretty warm. That late in the year, it should have been cold. I learned better coming back.

[We] went and landed at Marseille, but we went through the Straits of Gibraltar. And we got to see North Africa and Casablanca, things like that. Then we landed at Marseille. When we first got off the ship, we were carrying our baggage, a barracks bag and our packs and our rifles. We were like we were drunk, trying to keep our—you know, on the dock because we'd been rolling around in the ocean so long. We were—it was—then we marched up to our campsite and camped out and dug our holes and got ready and dinner prepared.

Well, we started up the Belfort Gap through the Rhône valley. That was right after the Eighth Air Force had been strafing where the Germans were pulling out. And that was a sight to behold because mile after mile after mile of their equipment, horse-drawn, horses and oxen in the field, you know, bloated up. That was the first— Just for two hundred miles or a hundred and fifty miles of it, endless. . . . [T]hey moved us in trucks and then, on December the sixteenth is when the Battle of the Bulge started. That's when it started freezing and getting cold and snow, even up in northern France—what do I want to say—up by Reims. [We] had our overcoats and regular gloves and our helmets and our little caps to pull down over our ears. One of the things we learned trucking up to the Third Army— We were assigned to Patton's army to relieve the Bulge at that time. We were all riding in trucks, and I— For some reason, we had number ten cans, and I put dirt in, got some gasoline, and we had a little fire in the truck. With it closed, it was pretty comfortable. But the next morning when we got out, we all were black with soot. It was comical.

• • •

The city of Dachau, the town of Dachau was a small country town. It was in a wedge in the road. I remember when we were riding the lead tank and we got some fire from the right front on the side of a hill. We didn't know it then, but there were some SSers dug in there. So we hopped off the tank, and there was a perfect ditch leading right up that road. We crossed at those trees at—I have a picture of it—and we had flat shooting, right in their holes. We shot them up—there were four to six of them—and killed them all, and we went on about our business, you know. And we stopped. They said, "We're going to hold up for the night, dig in."

But we went in this first house, and it was a real nice-looking house. I didn't know it at the time, but that was the doctor out at the camp, at Dachau. And his family—they had a sitting room, a kitchen, a basement, upstairs, and three or four bedrooms downstairs. Real nice farmhouse. The grandmother was there, the grandfather, the daughters—the family. There must have been six or seven of them. So we ran them out of there and let them stay in the basement. They had bacon and everything. They were cooking, frying bacon. I never will forget the Germans' counterattack. They were firing artillery. But anyhow, I set up a machine gun in that window, in that library. So we went about cooking, and I started frying some bacon. Here comes some artillery in, and you're pretty safe in a house, unless it's big artillery. One of those—piece of shrapnel went right through that frying pan, and the bacon grease caught fire on that stove and ruined our bacon grease for frying potatoes. Have to put the fire out. But later on, we found out that that was the doctor out at that camp. God knows what he pulled. The next morning, we were on the road again, and we came to the camp and the railroad sidings and things like that. You have some of those pictures of that.

[We came up to the camp along the railroad siding.] And to the right was the railroad and there were marshaling yards. There must have been seven, eight tracks across, and then the warehouses, whole long stretch of warehouses. About a hundred yards of warehouses. And that's where we first broke into the camp. And we weren't getting, we were getting some mortar fire intermittently. There was yelling and carrying on, and people were running.

[I noticed] the stink. It's a stench. But that wasn't from the gas ovens. Just human stench. Death stench. [We investigated the railcars.] . . . [T]here were three hundred—I think on one of those photographs are the amount—there were three hundred railcars full of dead, and they all looked the same. They had their striped suits on, and they just died in there, starved to death. But they opened some of the doors and—our company lieutenant had a camera, and he took pictures of several of those, and I have those original, old, little photographs of them.

. . . [T]hose that could walk, they were like walking skeletons. You can't believe that a person can walk that thin. It's just amazing. But the dead and things like that—they weren't embracing us, they were just yelling, and a lot of them were clustered up. Some of them brought some cans that they had gotten out of the German soldiers' canteen or barracks or whatever—you know, like our number ten cans—and I was—we spent a long time opening those cans. In fact, that bayonet, I wore my hands out cutting cans open. We didn't have can openers or anything. But it was for hours. We'd take turns.

[Before we got to Dachau, we hadn't heard of these sorts of

places.] Not one word, not one word, not one word. It was funny how they barracksed them, you know, like meal slots. They're living lengthwise in a hole, four or five of them in a hole. They're all stunk and dying and dead, crapping on themselves. Just— I guess that one day I saw more dead than the whole town of Galveston.

We stayed there that night. We dug in that night. But we went around, and I went and looked at the ovens. The chimneys, big stacks, were there. I looked at the ovens, and they had dead stacked to go in the ovens. They had kind of a roller system. They'd put them on a long kind of stretcher and roll them in. But I read that that was coal fire, and they quit doing that. But I saw the gas jets. That was gas fire. I don't know who said that was coal fire. It might have been both, but I saw the gas jets. When you— There were four ovens that I recall. I guess, if you put ten bodies on a roller—four ovens, that's forty. And if it took an hour to do it, to burn it, I try to think of how many—going twenty-four hours a day—how many people that could die, that'd burn in there. That's a lot. They had a lot stacked, ready to go.

. . . [There] was a lake, and I assumed it was around because it was a long ditch and there were a lot of bodies in there. They were throwing them in there.

• • •

[S]ome of the things that you don't realize—it always makes you wonder how could human beings do that to human beings? But worse than killing is the deprivation that he inflicted upon those people by starving them to death. The misery over years and years and years. And that I don't under— I haven't ever come to grips with. The other thing is that each one of those prisoners had a bucket or a can and that was their duty bag. That's what they carried. They ate out of it, they shit in it, they peed in it, and they didn't have any place to wash it. The privation that he inflicted— or they inflicted—not he, they—because there were plenty of people to blame. Because you could—you know, a blind man would see what was going on.

HERMAN "HANK" JOSEPHS

Excerpts from an interview conducted by Stephen M. Sloan

October 22, 2011

So I remember the Holocaust, which means 'remembrance,' so we remember the indignity suffered by so many different peoples—deaths and starvation and beatings and surgical instances.

. . . I have a confession to make. The first forty years I was married, I didn't say a word about it. It was too horrible to dredge up my memory. But then I—in twenty-oh-one [2001]—I wrote my autobiography so my kids would know what their father had gone through. And I have four children, a boy and three girls. And so I wanted them to know what I thought, where I was, where I've been, my situation, so that they would know.

• • •

My mother came with her four siblings to the United States in 1922, and I helped them celebrate their fiftieth anniversary here in this country at the St. Anthony Hotel in San Antonio. So I had a bunch of uncles and aunts, and I admired them all. They pulled themselves up by their bootstraps and were very successful. My father was in the dry-goods business, and he had a hard time making a living. But he believed in going where the money was, so he came to—first to Ingleside, then Refugio, then Kilgore, Texas, and then Corpus Christi, to the Saxet Field, which is *Texas* spelled backwards. So he came where the oil was, because that's where the money was. And he— We never missed a meal, and I'm very grateful.

I had a wonderful father, a wonderful mother. I was very fortunate. My father was an incurable romantic, as I am, and my mother was a businesswoman. She loved business, and she was very successful. She paid her bills on the first of the month like a clock. And she had been in charge of their grocery store in Zhitomir, which is near Kiev in Ukraine, in Russia. And she was twelve years old. When everybody else was out playing or going to synagogue, she was working. So my—that was my mother's benefit of life, was that she was the manager of their little grocery store that they had, where people were so poor, they used to come in and they used to buy one *kopek* of butter or a piece of bread. So when she married my dad, who was very romantic— They had met at a synagogue picnic, and they fell in love. And he wrote her poetry in Romanian. He was from Bucharest, Romania. His name was Josepovich originally. And wrote her poetry in Romanian, sang to her, and eventually married her. And I'm a product of that. I'm a progeny of that marriage, luckily. I'm lucky I had a well-educated father. He loved to read. Read all of the romantic writers of his time. And—that didn't prepare me for World War II.

So when I was sixteen years old, I started college. So I'd had two years in college by the time I was drafted at age eighteen, and first thing I knew, I was sent overseas. You know, after three months in the service, I was not prepared for what faced me, but all I knew was, Thou shalt not kill. And they stuck a rifle in my hand and said, Thou shall kill thy enemy. So we went to an unknown enemy, and we killed them.

I was inducted at Fort Sam Houston, San Antonio, 1944, in February, and I was sent to Camp Maxey, up near Weatherford, Texas, and went through basic training there—six-week basic. And we shipped over to England—Liverpool, landed in Liverpool, England. And we were training to invade Normandy. We didn't know it, but we were. And we trained, and it was so cold there it would freeze your head off up in Liverpool—near Liverpool. Nottingham was where we were. And the wind just whistled through those tents like there was nothing there. And there was a little stove in the center of the tent. It was an eight-man tent. And the wind just whistled through there, and there was a charcoal fire going, but that didn't help much. Couldn't take a shower, because the showers were outside, and it was cold, cold, cold, as only England can get cold. That's what I said then. Of course, it was colder in Belgium.

So from England, we took off from Bournemouth after a couple of months of training there. And we boarded a ship and, on June the fifth, 1944, we boarded a ship and took off for the French coast, and we landed and invaded Normandy, Omaha Beach. Followed the Second Ranger Battalion in. So we were the first ones on the beach, actually. And a sergeant friend of mine, a good friend of mine, he was the only Jewish fellow in my company. He got hit by bullets the moment we hit the beach. He said, "Don't worry, Tex. I'll get you up the beach. It's a walk in the park." It was the first time I'd heard that, too. So he got shredded. He got shot by— You know, a dozen bullets entered his body. He was dead. I laid down in back of him and heard the bullets thud into him. And when they stopped to reload, during the silence I got up and took off for the—the hill, which was about fifty feet high, of sand, where the Germans were, and pillboxes. And there were

sand traps and barbed wire and land mines, so I was damn lucky to get up there. And a company of engineers had put a bunch of TNT boxes in where the sand was the shallowest, and they blew it up to smithereens. And we went through there and into where the Germans were. And we killed them. We had fire-blowers and machine guns and we were— You either kill or be killed.

. . .

Well, do you want me to tell you that it was a beautiful day for a ride? We were atop the Bavarian mountains looking down at little villages, which gleamed in the sun. People were sweeping up the cobblestones. And we were told to go down and check on a little town near München, Munich, called Dachau. And we were on our way to Dachau to find out what was going on there. And we got there and the first thing we saw when we got to— to Dachau was a sign over the entrance which says "Work Will Make You Free." *Arbeit Macht Frei.* So we went through the gate there with three—about three dozen cabins. They had about fifty men each, I guess. And some trucks and some places we felt were gashouses, where people were gassed.

. . . I looked at the prisoners in their striped garb, so filthy and decimated. One of them moved, and I went over to him and he said, "*Bist a Yid?*" Are you Jewish? I said, "*Ich bin a Yid.*" I am Jewish. And then I told him, "*Alles geet. Alles geet.*" I speak a little Yiddish, which is pig-German. And—"*Alles geet. Alles geet.*" All is good. All is good. And I opened my C rations and fed him a little soup—made a little soup for him. And he died two hours later in my arms. And I asked him what his name was. He said, "*Meine namen ist Herman.*" "*Ich.*" My name is Herman, too. So I had tears in my eyes, and I cry every time I think about it. This poor guy, he was about forty years old and weighed about fifty pounds, maybe. And that's how much he had been maltreated.

That's a hell of a load for a young fellow, nineteen years old. It was May of 1945. And we went— Or late April. And that was when we went to Dachau. I had no idea that people—there were—so many people were in prison. Pentecostal people, priests, politicians, especially Jews had—behind bars, behind barbed wire, and treated like animals—worse than animals. There were beds there that—boards I might say. Hard boards they slept on. They were so tired when they got through working them that they just collapsed, I figured. So big, that's a hard load for a young fellow.

[I was sent to Dachau because] I was part of I&R, intelligence and reconnaissance. And they sent us down there to check and see what was going on. They knew about concentration camps, but we didn't. So then they sent us to investigate what was going on as far as concentration camps was concerned, and we found out quickly. It was a horrible experience. We had been through four battles already, and we thought we were immune from being shocked, but that was quite a shock. Blew—blew my mind. Had no idea such a thing existed.

When I entered the concentration camp, I figured when they said *Arbeit Macht Frei*—means "Work Makes You Free"—I said, "That's funny. That's odd because it's not true." But they made the people believe it. And they—they gassed them. They killed them, lots of them. And I kept thinking, there's so many wonderful lives wasted. Composers, artists, scientists were killed just because Hitler said, "We—we—all non-Aryans, we want to kill them." And he was hell on wheels. Non-Aryans—you're a non-Aryan, you weren't—the perfect race. The Germans thought they were. He inculcated that in them.

We saw about three dozen barracks and a few automobiles and gas chambers. And we knew what they were for. There were people lying in the gas chambers, dead. And they had a ravine—ravine there and they had piled the bodies in the ravine and put lye on them. [How] can one man be that way toward another man and call himself a human being? That's more of an animal than a human being.

• • •

[I]t made me very proud to be able to say that I helped liberate a concentration camp. It made me a little different from other people who did not have that privilege, so that's the way I felt about it. I felt very proud to have done it, to have held a guy in my arms until he passed away, see what war can do. It made me hate war.

GERD MILLER

Excerpts from an interview conducted by Stephen M. Sloan

July 9, 2013

I was born [in Cologne, Germany] in '22. And fortunately, my father was far-sighted enough to see what was coming. We knew a little bit about the political situation because my dad was kind of a fan of radios when they were still fairly new and pretty high-tech. And at night we would get earphones, and you would listen to Radio Luxembourg or German-language from England, German-language from Italy, from France, Holland, and so forth. You took your life in your hands because if they found out that you were listening to foreign broadcasts, that was it. That was it. So we knew a little bit. He contacted his uncle here in the United States, applied for exit visa, and the uncle filled out all the necessary US papers. Actually it was his uncle's son. So his cousin filled out all the papers. Eventually, we went through the waiting period until the US quotas came up. We got our visa.

We left Germany in May of 1938: my father, my mother, myself, and a girl, who was my double cousin. And we went to Rotterdam, in Holland. It was all so very difficult, not only to get a permit to leave Germany. In fact, my father lost everything he had there. When he arrived in the United States, he had twenty-four dollars. But he had another cousin who married a man who was on the board of directors of the Holland America Line, who was not Jewish. They lived in Rotterdam. And through that connection, he was able to get passage on a ship. . . . We got off in Houston, Texas. And my father's cousin had arranged for us to live in Seguin because his father, at one time, had a little country store there in the center of Seguin. And so we went to Seguin. They decided to send me to high school so that I would have an American high school diploma. It was pretty tough learning the language. But there were a lot of Germans in Seguin, and we got along pretty well.

• • •

When I tried to join the American army after Pearl Harbor, they told me, "You can't join our army. You're an enemy alien." Because I was—technically, here I was considered a German. In Germany, the Jews were not considered German anymore. Then I tried to go—tried the navy; tried to get into the National Guard. The National Guard was doing close-order drill in the basement of the San Antonio Auditorium, the city auditorium. And I went down there. And I talked to some old noncom [noncommissioned officer]. And he said, "Well, you're an enemy alien. You can't join our forces." But he said, "One thing you could do." He said, "You can volunteer to allow them to draft you." I said,

"Whatever it takes," you know. I signed some paper. And it took, maybe, six months, and I got my draft notice.

Dachau was the first concentration camp that the Nazis put up, I think in 1935. . . . And when we came, when the American army came there, people kept saying, "Well, we don't know anything about it." Believe me, I can tell you truly, that was pure b.s. Everybody knew about it. They wanted them to know about it because the threat was, "You open your mouth, you wind up in Dachau." At that time, it was a small camp. And it became fairly large. It was built, I think, to hold five thousand prisoners. When we liberated it, there were thirty-two thousand people in there.

They said, "We need every German-speaking soldier to go to Dachau." And I knew right away what Dachau was because I knew it since I was a kid. But I never suspected to find what we did there. I mean it was—I can't begin to tell you. It was hell on earth. I mean, it was like Dante's *Inferno*. We came in there shortly after these two units liberated the camp. We had to drive from Munich into Dachau, which was north-northwest. It took us about twenty minutes. It's not very far up, maybe ten miles. When we approached the village of Dachau, the smell—the smell was so awful. Now, we had all been in combat. And we had all seen and smelled dead soldiers, dead cows and horses. Nothing like what we found there. We came to the gate. The Americans that had gone in there, they had—I think they bulldozed through the gate or ran a tank through there or something. The camp was completely enclosed in high-tension wire. And somebody had cut that power out, but we found like half a dozen guys hanging in there. They had committed suicide by jumping on to the live wire. And I tell you, this may sound bad, but they were the lucky ones. What we found in that camp.

First of all, like I say, the smell of all those bodies, those rotting bodies. They were stacked all over the place. The people that were moving around, they were like skeletons. I mean, they were like zombies. They—most of them—a lot of them didn't have shoes, and they wore those blue and gray concentration camp outfits. Undernourished, covered with sores, teeth missing. A lot of them couldn't even move. They were laying on the ground. They waved to us, said something. A lot of foreigners there. You know, not everybody there was German. They were French. They were Russian, Polish, Yugoslav. I mean— But when we came in there, we didn't know what— I mean, it was so stunning and so

unbelievable. They had a gas chamber there, which we found later. And they had an oven, two ovens, those crematoriums. And they had run out of fuel, so people kept dying. I mean, I think they gave them eight hundred calories a day and worked them fourteen hours a day. These people were living skeletons and sick and weak. And their eyes were sunk. And they [were] covered with lice. And we had—well, later some of the medics finally came in there. Right near the main gate there were these administration buildings where the Nazis lived. And they were beautiful. Nice buildings, neat. They had a flower garden. And we knew right away, if there's any documents—you know, these guys took off—that's where we're going to find them.

But we wanted to go through the camp first to see what we could do for those people. The most frustrating thing was, what could we do for them? I mean, the American GI, they see these poor starving people. They reach in and gave them their K rations. They gave them food. An officer came and . . . said, "Do not give them food." He said, "They can't take that food. They haven't had a decent meal in months." All they got every day—they had these big kettles over a fire, and they got, like, a soup that was like—I would say 90 percent water and cabbage, and some kind of crap in there. And then they got a piece of dry bread. That's all they got to eat. Those people, they were weighing ninety, a hundred pounds.

. . . And the last thing we saw—in fact, one of the Frenchmen told me in French, "Have you seen the *chemin de fer*?" The railroad. I said no. That was way in the back, where the railroad track came in. And that's where we found thirty-nine cars full of bodies. It— I mean, it was so unbelievable. We didn't know what to do with those people. They had dysentery. They had—some of them had typhoid fever. They had sores all over their faces. They were undernourished and worked to death. Some of them were barefoot. Some of them had some of those wooden shoes. Some of them had nothing. A lot of them were just laying there on the ground, unable to move. And then a medical unit finally came in. They made more announcements. They said, "Be sure and don't give them food." Because in the C rations, if you opened that up, there was a big hunk of cheese. They couldn't take it. There was meat, Spam, I think, or something like that. There were powdered eggs. And these people were starving. I mean, they would eat—they would eat the weeds that were growing there just to get something into their stomach.

The medics finally set up some kind of a, I guess you would call it a mess hall, big cooking pots. And they brewed some kind of, some kind of soup for these prisoners. And then they used some of our tin cups to let them drink. And they told them, "Very slowly." And then we gave them bread. They called it cake. You know, we had that white bread. Well, in Europe the bread that they got was the ordinary bread, and half of it was wood chips, sawdust. So they called our bread cake. And they said, "Eat it very slowly, and dip it in that soup. Let your stomachs get used to it." And then more and more medics came in. I don't know from what unit.

So by that time we had seen enough. And I'll tell you something: I saw American soldiers just collapse and crying, throwing up. Really, nobody knew—what do you do? How do you help these people? So our officer, the senior officer said, "Let's get in these buildings and get a hold of all the documents and records." Because we found out, one of the things that happened in Dachau, they did these medical experiments on the prisoners. There was—and I have a list here of the names, which I will give you in a minute. One of the first ones was they did experiments on malaria, on how to treat malaria. So they intentionally infected hundreds and hundreds of prisoners with malaria. And then tried different treatments, most of which didn't work. I spoke to a prisoner who was in pretty good shape but wore the prison outfit. He was a doctor. He was from Czechoslovakia. The Nazis had him do autopsies of all the people that died. He was forced to do that. I forgot what he told me, how many thousand autopsies he had to do, people that died from the malaria experiments.

Then, they did experiments on people on how they—for the Luftwaffe—how they would survive in freezing water. They threw them into a container that had ice blocks floating in there and took their temperature every two minutes, and the people were screaming and hollering and freezing to death. And then they put some of these flying suits on that they were testing. And some of them protected them a little against that, but most of them didn't. And there were hundreds and hundreds of those people that just didn't survive, and if they were halfway alive later, they killed them. Then they did another set of experiments on explosive decompression. That was for the Luftwaffe also, because we found all those records later. That's how we knew. But we also heard from some of the prisoners. They would put them into a compression chamber and gradually increase the pressure like they would have in those planes. And then they would very suddenly drop the compression to simulate explosive decompression. But most of those people died, if not instantly, miserably. You know, their blood was boiling and it was so horrible.

Then we found our way to Linz, and on the other side of Linz was that huge concentration camp, Mauthausen. There were even more prisoners than Dachau, and it looked just like Dachau. Bodies stacked everyplace. The survivors walking around, you know, skin and bones. . . . And one of the worst things in Mauthausen— It's hilly country. They had a big cliff there. Like a two-hundred-foot cliff. And when the Nazis couldn't bury the bodies fast enough—kill the people fast enough—they'd push them off that cliff. Down below there were just tons of bodies laying there.

Those poor guys—thousands—they were dumped in a ditch with a bulldozer and covered up at the foot of that cliff in Mauthausen. The bodies were just stacked, rotten, rats running through there. It was just as bad. And, of course, now we know the Nazis had hundreds of those camps.

• • •

Later we went back, and we interviewed a number of the survivors from the camp that were able to tell us names, these doctors, and who did what and even some of the guards. And some of the guys that were in charge of some of the barracks that were— Don't forget, besides the political prisoners, there were a lot of criminals in there. And the Nazis put those criminals in charge of a barracks. And it is just—that one human being can do this to another. Including like in those thirty-nine cars, children, women—children—they let them die there. They either shot them or machine-gunned them or let them die from exposure and starvation. I will never understand, never understand—a country like Germany; educated people, you know. How could this happen? I don't know. I don't know to this day, how can they be that gullible? How can they be that uninformed? But a lot of them saw things that were going on and they looked the other way. Maybe they didn't participate, but they looked the other way.

CHESTER "CHET" ROHN
Excerpts from an interview conducted by Stephen M. Sloan

December 14, 2011

[We had some idea about what was happening in Europe.] Yeah, to some extent, but— In fact, I had even heard one of Hitler's speeches, in German, they put on the radio. But it didn't make that much impression. Yeah, Roosevelt said, "We're not going to war," so we believe him. But the war really didn't affect us. We were just coming out of the Depression. I think the war was responsible because all of our [heavy industry]—we were part of the buildup there, all of the heavy machinery. And Allis Chalmers, A. O. Smith, all these big companies were really producing for England. So we knew that was going on, but the war was a long way away. There was no television. Whatever you knew, you got from the newspaper or radio. And the war made some impression on us, but not that much. It did later on.

December of '41, that changed. I was in college by that time. University of Wisconsin in Madison. I was in chemical engineering, if you can imagine. . . . My dad said to me, "What do you think you'd like to take?" I said, "I don't know." So he said, "You know, engineering's a pretty good field." And I'd had a lot of math and science in high school, but—so I said, "Well, that sounds good to me." So I started out twenty-one credits as a freshman. And it was—I—it was way over my head. But now the war is starting

to come on. And of course, every day, every weekend there was a party for somebody who was leaving for the service. And I got to the end of my first semester of my sophomore year. And my dad knew the guy on the draft board, so he knew exactly when I was going to be called. And he worked it out so I could finish that semester. So then I was called, and off I went.

During the Bulge, we were infantry. Everybody was infantry. We were so shorthanded, and they had lost so many men between Normandy and Bastogne. There was an awful lot of heavy fighting and heavy losses. So they needed more bodies. And we were getting these poor guys that had been in the army maybe six weeks, and they sent them to us. They barely knew how to fire their rifle. And it was terrible because these guys were some of the first casualties over there.

The worst part was the weather. I think that was worse than the enemy because it went below zero for a while there in late December, and we didn't have winter clothing. And we didn't have winter shoes, you know. We just had our shoe boots. I mean, it's like a shoe, only with a high top on it that lapped over. And these were no good for that kind of weather. And we had wool uniforms, but it wasn't padded or anything else. And we finally got shoe packs which had a felt insole and was much warmer, but that was after most of the cold weather was gone. [To stay warm], well, the first thing you did when there were a lot of pine needles, you took your bayonets and we'd slash low branches and put that down for our bed, maybe get pine needles this thick on the bottom of our hole. And I wasn't in individual foxholes. We had to dig a machine-gun foxhole because I had my assistant gunner with me. So that was kind of like a shape here, the gun was there, and we'd get around this way and then that way, which was kind of nice with two of us because one of us could sleep while the other stood guard. But most of the cold—we learned the cold comes from the bottom, not just from the top. And you better be— You know, you can have all the blankets you want on top of you, but you got to have insulation below. And that's what the pine needles, pine branches did. So we would really make a bed. And I think I only had one blanket to put over. But at least down in the hole you didn't have the wind. It was a little warmer down there and you could finally fall asleep.

But the living conditions were the worst part of it. Absolute worst part of it. You were always cold, plus you were always tired. There were some times, if we had two or three hours of sleep in two or three days, we were lucky. And you could be talking to somebody and they'd fall asleep talking to you on their feet. And this happened to all of us. We were exhausted, dirty. I had two showers in almost five months. They only— There'd be a big ring around your mouth as far as your tongue could go; you could clean this part. The rest of us, we hadn't shaved, didn't want to shave because it was too cold. But the bath would be out in the middle of a field, and they'd give you a shower in this weather. In Belgium, as I said, it was zero sometimes, or below. I don't know how cold but, oh, ice everywhere, snow everywhere. And they said, "All right, you guys, you're going to get a shower today." . . . That meant going out in the middle of a field. They would put—I don't know what they had, but it wasn't a tent for going around like this because the guy giving you the shower is up on a ladder above you. And you had— They gave you thirty seconds, I think, to soap up and another thirty seconds to dry. And here you are, stark naked, and just this canvas around here. And then you got to get outside and dry. . . . But other than that, we were dirty. The filth was—you were just caked with dirt. But so was everybody else, you know. And why we didn't get more—I did get dysentery over there, by the way. And I was stuck in a German block house for about three or four days. I've never been

so darn sick in my life—but why we didn't have more people get that. And it was from drinking water out of a stream. There probably was a dead horse ten yards up the stream or something. So the living conditions, to me, were the worst part of the war.

And then they gave us mittens. First, they gave us nothing. We had, I don't know, some little thin thing. But this was a big, leather thing. Three fingers went here, and then they had a finger hole for here and a thumbhole here. There was—only problem was they didn't get together with the rifle manufacturers to figure out your trigger finger could not go in the trigger housing of a rifle. So when we're out on patrol at night—I mean, you know, it was kind of spooky. And I was not going to not be able to fire if I had to. I mean, you'd see a tree and you'd swear it was moving or something like that. Walking on, we were silent, no noise. We even took the stacking swivels off our rifles because they would clank. So, anyway, here you are; my left hand was fine; I kept that big mitten on.

. . .

We had heard about these camps, but we didn't know much about them. We knew there were camps; we knew that way back. There were concentration camps. And we heard their prisoners were being killed and all that. But it didn't really register till we started seeing the dead prisoners in the striped uniforms all along the road, coming from the north down to Mauthausen. And I hadn't seen any of that anywhere else in Germany until we got . . . right along the Czech border. . . . [W]e started seeing more and more of these bodies lying around the ditches. And I mean dozens and dozens and dozens. And we—what's going on? What?—and then we figure, okay, they're concentration camp prisoners. Why are they killing them here? So the day after liberation, I was in Mauthausen. And I don't know how to explain it, but it was the— First of all, you could smell it way before you got there. The corpses around there. They had what they called the hospital yard, and it was what they—where they put people that were dying. Nothing to keep the weather out, you know. You just stay behind this barbed wire till you die. And I'd go—we'd stand, and these people would stare at you with a blank look, and all you could do is stare back. We had— Some prisoners who could speak English acted as guides. I mean, they took us into the gas chamber, and they took us into the morgue or whatever it is, where they knocked the gold teeth out. And so we saw all that. They took us to the crematorium. We were in that. And in the barracks.

And some of these guys were imprisoned because they were newspaper people from Czechoslovakia; anybody that was against the Nazi regime. Mauthausen was built back in the thirties, not as a concentration camp but as a prison for German civilians and I think also to provide a labor source because all— they had a big—I don't know, limestone or granite or whatever they—they say that the city of Vienna was built with stone from Linz. And they had one of the big quarries there. And all the prisoners finally did that, but early on these were just German prisoners, you know. It looked more like a big federal prison than the pictures you see of Auschwitz, which were all these hundreds of barracks and out in the open. This was a big stone edifice and everything else. But they had a bunch of crummy barracks in there, too, where they'd put in, like, four or five to a bed.

And it ended up just being a death camp. Anybody that went to Mauthausen wasn't ever going to get out. . . .

And the camp hadn't been cleaned up. Our bulldozers had to bury the people and the bulldozer just pushing the bodies into a trench. There were so many—I don't know how many were dead when we got there. It seemed everywhere you looked there were dead people, some of them stacked up. The crematorium wasn't big enough. They couldn't burn them fast enough. So that's why we ended up burying them in trenches that were a hundred yards long. It was just—just awful.

They were just living skeletons. You'd look at somebody—the guy just be standing there, stark naked, on the other side of the barbed wire, and he'd just look at you with these vacant eyes. And you didn't know what to say to him or anything. His knees looked like this because everything else— I could have put my hand around a guy's thigh or here, with my fingers. And their hips were huge and their knees were huge and their heads were huge, and their rib cages stuck out all over. It was—their waists, about that big around. I couldn't believe some of them were alive that I saw standing there. I thought, "How could anybody even be alive?" You know, maybe they weighed forty, fifty, sixty pounds. And you looked at them and they were probably guys that weighed 180 at one time, or 190 pounds. It was terrible.

Disease—luckily we'd all had all kinds of shots, so we didn't get sick, but there was typhus and typhoid and you name it. They were dying from everything you can think of. It was something so different than we had been used to seeing. We saw a lot of dead Germans and a lot of dead Americans, but nothing like this. It's almost impossible to describe. And together with the smell, it was unbelievable. We couldn't believe it. We just couldn't believe it. But there it was.

Well, they wanted us to see what they were doing. He said nobody—you know, unless they see it, they're not going to believe it. I don't know. I just don't have words to tell you how bad it was.

• • •

[In 2010], we took a "battle tour." [W]e covered the whole—and I don't know how many hundred miles it is from Bastogne down to Linz, but I'm sure it's got to be four hundred anyway. It was a fifteen-day tour, but the first couple of days we went there, we went to the different cemeteries. . . . [We went back to Mauthausen on that trip.] We ended in Mauthausen on the ceremony of the sixty-fifth anniversary of its liberation. That was all timed so it worked out. And all these people came from all over. They had a parade of people—we had all these VIP seats that they put out for the old gaffers. And these—parade of people came with their flags and huge wreaths of flowers to put on—I don't even know what it was, some kind of memorial. . . . And delegations came from all over the world. Some, there were only four or five people; others, there were twenty, thirty people. It was very impressive. And all of them had had their nationals as prisoners—even China, which surprised me. But it was a—it was very impressive.

And we had our, as I say, our own ceremonies there. And met an awful lot of people; there're just so many people. And I've got people I still want to see. . . . [One gentleman came up to thank me there at the ceremony.] He came up to me and I knew he was American—dressed in a suit and the way he talked. But I'd never seen him before. And he came up and just—all he said was, "Thank you for saving my wife." And I thought, "What wife did I save?" You know, it didn't register at first. And then, later, I found out he was the husband of one of the babies born in Mauthausen.

HERBERT U. STERN

Excerpts from an interview conducted by Stephen M. Sloan

May 31, 2012

I feel—it is so important since so many survivors, either Holocaust survivors or people like myself, feel that we're at the end of our lives and possibly, in another few years, there are no so-called eyewitnesses that have been through all this. Since you're talking about the Holocaust itself—over six million people that died in one form or another plus the huge casualties during World War II—that I think it's so important for younger generations to at least have some knowledge that in past—many years prior to all this—World War I, Civil War, whatever the wars that you've had—that you have the benefit of a lot more detailed recordings for history that were not to that extent available. I've studied a lot about the Civil War. I minored in history and majored in economics in college and continued to be interested to a great extent in oral history. So I feel that the—anything that we do in publicizing that period which was so traumatic in the thirties and forties and even into the fifties is, I hope, of a great deal of benefit for future generations.

I arrived in this country on August 26, 1936, to New York and was met by . . . my uncle and his wife in New York and stayed with them for about a week at that particular time. Talk about sweating it out. I was staying with my father's closest friend, who was an attorney. His entire family died at Auschwitz. My sister—when the Germans marched into the Sudetenland of Czechoslovakia, they fled to Prague. My aunt and her family first were taken to—flew to Italy temporarily and then to England. My sister was on the last plane out of Prague before the Germans marched in.

I didn't realize, obviously, at the time that my moving in 1936—how lucky I really was to be able to start a whole new life. We had nothing to look forward to in any way, shape, or form. It was just a dead end for us. It was almost like being snared somewhere. You know, you're in a maze and you can't get out. You felt sooner or later you would be taken away. It wasn't that long thereafter. There were—I think in the midthirties there were people who just plain disappeared. And you never heard from them again. To tell you that, if you were in an apartment building and you looked downstairs, particularly on weekends, and you'd see thousands and thousands of brown shirts marching. They were always just doing—the SA and SS were always marching in these huge formations. You may have seen pictures of Nuremburg where they had a hundred thousand uniformed people and Hitler speaking to them and this kind of thing. We all saw this, whether it was on the news or in pictures or actually in person. It was frightening, because you felt this was a new force.

• • •

At the time I set foot in Nordhausen in March 1945, I had no specific knowledge of slave labor or extermination camps. On the other hand, in the mid-1930s, while I still lived in Berlin, we heard instances where prominent Jewish residents of Berlin were taken away by the Gestapo in the middle of the night. In some instances, they were released after brief periods of detention in Berlin. Others disappeared. Around 1940–41 (I was then in the US about to enter the US Army) some of us heard about what came to be known much later as concentration camps. My father had written from England that he had received word that a number of cousins and my maternal grandmother had been sent to a detention camp in a town called Auschwitz in Poland. Unfortunately, no one ever heard from them again. By 1942, it became known to the Allies that "The Final Solution" had been instituted by the Nazi High Command. This was the expanding roundup of thousands of Jews, political opponents, Gypsies, and homosexuals, and others, not only in Germany but also in the newly occupied countries. I also remember, in 1942 in England, my father knew friends who owned shortwave radios that picked up the daily clandestine French Resistance Calais calling, and, on occasions, they heard of mass killings in camps. But not until the camps were liberated in 1945 did anyone become aware of the extent of the barbarities that were taking place.

• • •

From a separate testimony submitted to the Texas Holocaust and Genocide Commission:

The capture of Nordhausen Slave Labor Camp April 1945. To the best of my recollection, the American First Army—its VII Corps had no specific plans to "liberate" the Nordhausen slave labor camp. For historic purposes, the events in which I was involved and will describe took place during the period of April 11 to April 14, 1945.

I was a member of the Ninth Infantry Division and assigned to the G2 Section of the Division. Since I spoke German and French (I was born in Berlin, Germany, and lived there until age sixteen. I escaped from Germany in 1936 and came to the US to live with distant relatives in Cincinnati, Ohio), much of my work in the division was interrogation, document interpretation, and in liaison assignments with Battalion S-2's, medical field personnel, engineers, etcetera. Some of these assignments were in forward combat areas. (I was twice wounded in combat.) In specific instances, there were contacts with resistance fighters in Normandy and, at times, I was on detached service in Tunisia and Algeria with native Goumiers under the command of Free French forces, actually also called Corps Franc d'Afrique.

Between April 11 and April 12, 1945, we were clearing pockets of resistance in the Ruhr industrial areas. At one point, an estimated 30,000 German soldiers surrendered to us. The newest assignment was to start a 150-mile motor march to the Harz-Nordhausen area. In this area, remnants of the Eleventh SS *Panzer* Army was bottled up, refusing to surrender. German High Command had also formed three new divisions. They too were among the holdouts. Two elite divisions began facing the Ninth.

The Harz Mountains had few equals for national fortifications: approximately twenty-two miles across and sixty-eight miles long, up to 4,000 feet, excellent observation posts. Unquestionably, the Hitler government chose this area to become a highly industrialized enterprise. According to my recollection, the First Army planned to bypass the Harz Mountain Fortress then encircle the area. The reduction of this pocket constituted the last major obstacle facing the VII Corps of which we were a part.

As we were motoring, mostly in two-and-a-half-ton trucks, towards the town of Nordhausen, we came upon a railroad yard and saw, on flatcars, fins and other large components of V-2 Rockets. Approximately a quarter-mile from the railroad yard was a well-camouflaged entrance to a mountain tunnel. Inside the tunnel were rows of highly placed electrical lights. We could also see small-gauge railroad tracks, long steel tables, some benches, scattered chains, and other unidentified paraphernalia. There were no signs of human beings inside the tunnel. I recall that we walked about 400 to 500 yards to the slave labor camp coming face to face with one of Germany's most notorious concentration camps. The carnage and horror had been uncovered earlier that day by tankers of the Third Armored Division and infantrymen of the 104th Division.

Here, the living and the dead were lying side by side. The living were too emaciated to move their limbs. The dead were unburied or half-buried. SS troops had stacked bodies in ditches. The stench was unbelievable. Many of us threw up. Yet, we took photos with newly acquired cameras (while fighting on the Ruhr, we uncovered a German AGFA plant with large inventories of new cameras, tripods, and lenses). We learned that one group which could not walk had been chained in the mountain tunnel for three months without seeing daylight. I also spotted a bank of very large ovens on the premises. There was no doubt that camp personnel burned the dead in these ovens. On the grates, you could see bones.

I recall that we commandeered the mayor of nearby Nordhausen to round up able-bodied men to dig additional long trenches to bury the skeletal bodies. I also remember that several townspeople exclaimed that they knew nothing about the slave labor camp. This infuriated us even more at the time.

In due time, we learned that Nordhausen had a long, drawn-out system of torture. One method was to crowd several hundred prisoners into a courtyard. There, on a raised platform, the condemned were hanged. Others were taken to the mountain tunnel, chained to work benches, and worked to death or beaten to death. They were there to assemble parts of the V-2 Rockets. Almost all prisoners were simply starved to death.

It is of course well known that the British Royal Air Force in 1942 bombed the original V-2 Rocket assembly and launch facilities in Peenemünde on the Baltic Sea. The entire program was obviously moved to the Harz Mountains. The prisoners of this notorious camp were French, Russians, Poles, Lithuanians, Romanians. I'm not certain that any Jews were at that camp.

Somewhat later, I learned that US field hospital facilities were temporarily stationed at the camp to minister to those who were still alive and could be treated there.

Considering that we had been through eight major campaigns in combat, 1942–1945, Nordhausen slave labor camp was the most traumatic experience we encountered.

JOHN VALLS

Excerpts from an interview conducted by Stephen M. Sloan

March 2, 2012

I took basic training in Amarillo. I took the test for pilot. I was—always loved airplanes—or model airplanes. I passed it. I marched in in 1944. I stayed there until March. They eliminated us without prejudice. We didn't do anything wrong. The whole school was gone because they had too many pilots. I went before a colonel and he says, "What do you feel like?" I said, "Well, sir—" He says—and then he told me, "I'm going to send you to a gunnery school. You're going to be a gunner in an airplane." And I said, "Sir—" I thought I'd impress him. I said, "Sir, if I can't fly the airplane, nobody's going to fly it for me." He didn't say anything, wrote something down, and then he said, "Next."

The next day I was in the infantry. They transferred me to the infantry. They sent me to Reno, Nevada. I did nothing but went out in a truck in the sand and stayed in a tent. They were training us to go to North Africa. Fortunately, I got my orders changed, I don't know why. They sent me to Greensboro, North Carolina. There, I was in a track meet. I won everything. Then they sent me to Boston. I shipped out of Boston, fourteen days to Southampton, England. Out of the fourteen days I was seasick thirteen. [I'd never been on the ocean before.] And you had a bunk and the—if you were lucky you got the top bunk, because the guy at the top would vomit and it would come all the way down. And it would—it happened. It happened. Oh God, I suffered. Oh!

But we got to England and, sure enough, that episode where—I . . . found a field, beautiful track field, with hurdles and all. I went and ran there. A man, a very well dressed man, saw me. I know it was him because when I got back to the base, Base Air Depot Number Two, we were taking infantry training. They said, "Hey, the colonel wants to see you." I went in, saluted him. What the heck did I do? And he said, "They want you to go run in London." I said, "Yes, sir, that's fine." They flew me in a C-47 all by myself into London, and that's when the—they told us, "Hey, the queen is going to be here. We want you British subjects to stand before— When she comes out, you will bow like this. And you, Yank, you don't have to bow but you can stand at attention." But everything was—I mean, the queen was like a god to them. It was—and I got the fever, too, when everybody came and when she came out. And I bowed, too, just like the rest of them. But I won. I won the four-hundred-meter hurdles. I'd never run the four-hundred-meter hurdles before. . . . So the next week the colonel called me in: "They want you to go to someplace else." I forget where. And I went and again I won. And the third week it's, again, C-47 to another meet, and again I won and they gave me a prize and everything. I sent the prizes to Laredo and they got here.

In one of them I had a certificate, was signed by a bunch of lords. I got it somewhere. I think it's in one of those books that my daughter made of me. And it said, "This medal will be given to you when obtainable." This was during the war, so I understood that. And this was in, I think, March? No. Well—August. August of 1944? Yeah, '44. I found the certificate in August '94, and I sent it to the ambassador for the United States here, in Washington. Oh, he sent me a very nice letter. "Please refer your request to—" some town in England. So I did the same things: "When do I get my medal?" And they wrote back, says, "We have received your inquiry with great interest. We will be in touch." In about two weeks they sent me the medal. It was really something.

• • •

And we had a lesson that we had to say the words "Kill or be killed." "Kill or be killed." Thirty times a day we had to say it. Anytime we met a buddy and just, "Kill or be killed." And Patton— I never—I didn't see him. The sergeant gave us—or the captain or somebody gave us the—said, "You will not surrender. You will die, but you will not surrender. You will not retreat. You might die, but you will not retreat. Understand that." And sure enough, finally I get to see my first German soldier in combat, face to face. And I couldn't shoot him. I couldn't kill him because I turned cold. I turned cold and I couldn't shoot him. He threw his gun down and surrendered. Ooh, I took him in. I said, "I caught a Nazzy! I caught a Nazzy!" I didn't even know how to pronounce *Nazi*. And I told the sergeant, "Sarge, I couldn't kill him. I turned cold." He says, "Don't worry, son. Next time you won't." And sure enough, it was—oh! From that day on, it was rough. It was bad.

I was only a PFC [private first class], but I was the leader. Everybody followed me, even in my half-track. Everybody followed me, what I did. I told them what to do and they did. And the master sergeant was in charge of us and he gave us the instructions every day, but the first guy that— When I finally got

to France, a captain, I forget his name, but he told me, "I'm your CO [commanding officer] here and I don't wear my bars because it's nothing but an aiming stick." Sure enough, in four days he was killed. Out of a company of twenty-two that I joined with, two of us from the original came back. It was—it was hell. It was really hell.

And you try to tell kids, you've got to dig a hole every night, whether it's raining, snowing, or whatever. You got to dig a hole, because if you were above the ground, mortars come and hand grenades come, and they go this way and that way. So, I mean, every night. Many times we took houses; we took towns that didn't fight. We had an American officer that spoke German. Every time we got to a town, he'd say, "If you fire one shot at us, we will destroy your town. If you don't fire at us, we're not going to disturb you. We're not going to fire either. So please surrender and avoid bloodshed," and whatever. Sometimes we went in, no problems. Sometimes we went in and kids with *Panzerfaust*, rifles with hand grenades—boom! boom!—beat the hell out of us. And it was— We lost a lot of people. You didn't make friends. You did not make friends because your friend was gone the next day.

And I got wounded. I don't have the Purple Heart, but I got wounded in my leg and in my arm. If I hadn't been wearing my helmet, I would have been killed. The thing exploded on top of us. I feel pling, pling, pling, pling, pling! And the guy next to me, the Polack: "I'm hit! I'm hit!" He was covered with blood, all the—all in front. And so, "Hey, medic! Medic!" So they went and got him, took him off. And the next day they brought him back with a Band-Aid. He had been hit right here (*laughs and gestures at neck*), nothing but a little thing but enough for blood to— He was mad as hell. I remember it. And that night, all of us tried to take our jackets off and mine wouldn't. The blood. The jacket had stopped the blood. And in my leg, too. But we didn't say any— I don't have the Purple Heart, but I was wounded.

But this is—that's another beautiful thing too. Number one, I'd lie in my hole at night and see thousands of bombers coming over; thousands, thousands, thousands coming over. I said, "God, we cannot lose this war," because there was doubt when we went in. The United States was number seven in power. Germany was first, England was second, France was third, Italy was fourth, Japan was fifth, and somebody else—I forget—Italy or whatever. We were number seven. We didn't know that we could win the war, but we did. . . . But towards the end we were so tired—mentally, not physically. We were strong—but so tired mentally that I prayed, and so did everybody else, to get killed or get this goddamn war over with. And that's also the exact word. Please, please, I've had it. I don't see the end. I don't see the end. I'm here and I can't do anything about it. I'm hungry, I'm scared, I'm tired, I'm cold. It was bad, bad, bad, bad. You cannot imagine.

• • •

We didn't know anything about the camps. I learned about [Hermann] Goering and [Joseph] Goebbels and all those after the war. I didn't know. I was just a kid from high school that really was very naïve. I didn't know anything. No. But when I saw that, I thought, "How can any people do that to other people? How— It's impossible. It's impossible!"

I don't even remember what the orders were for that day. I know that we were under [Field Marshal Bernard] Montgomery. We were not— The Ninth Armored Division had been loaned to Montgomery, but we were still taking orders from my sergeant. My sergeant told me, "Hey, patrol this area and go into this area." And I was alone, mind you, and I walked and I saw a giant wall right by, right on the street. And I said, "This is strange." I didn't know it was a prison camp. I opened the gate. It wasn't even locked. I opened the gate, and . . . I walked in and everybody was looking at me. Everybody was standing, and there were some people in racks that I could see. They were laying down just— and all they did was got their heads up and looked and came right back down. They were dying. They were—and it stunk. It was very—

And all of a sudden this man comes up to me and tells me [unintelligible ululating]. He was trying to give me his prize possession, which was a sleeveless rabbit skin coat. I said, "No, no, no, I can't. I'm an American soldier. I can't take anything. Go, you're free! You're free. Go!" But then very soon thereafter the English came in, and I understand that— *Life* magazine was also there because I've got the magazine that shows the pictures that

they took. And Eisenhower got the people in the town to come and parade down and see what—the atrocities. There was about five thousand bodies on the street, all just dead. I never saw anything like that. It was gruesome. It was— As a matter of fact, I wanted to get the hell out of there because I couldn't, number one, I couldn't stand the smell; and number two, there was already some British soldiers coming in after me. And they were in charge. Let them be in charge. I don't want to have anything to do—and I went on and—but now I know where I was, and I know that *Life* magazine was there the next day. But it was gruesome.

• • •

I was— I know one thing. I know I have a guardian angel. I know it. I know it. I've been in so many bad things that somebody did speak for me, even now. Even now . . . And it's— I've got a guardian angel, I hope.

MELVIN E. WATERS

Excerpts from an interview conducted by Stephen M. Sloan

I was a senior in high school when—sixteen years old when the war started. I remember December the sixth well. And I was so upset and all that I wanted to quit school and go in the navy, because I always heard of these underaged guys getting in the navy, and see the world. And my mother said, "I am not signing any papers for you until you have to go. You've got to wait for the draft."

I left college early. I went home for Thanksgiving. Never did go back. I went down to the Marine Corps recruiting office with a friend of mine that I played football with. And he was going to join the Marine Corps, so I went down with him and saw him off. It was one of those deals where—I don't know where his parents were, but it was one of those deals where he went down, took a physical, and left that night. So I went down and held his hand, and they talked me into taking a physical. And so I told my parents about it and my mother said, "You're not going anywhere. I'm not going to sign papers for you." So I was home, and I was going to start school in the second semester taking business administration. And my dad told me, he said, "If you want to go into the Marine Corps, you can." And I said, "Mother won't sign

the papers." He said, "Well, let me work on that." So finally he talked her into signing my papers and I went up. And, of course, I had taken a physical along with my friend in the latter part of November. I went up and left to go to San Diego on January the second. And then when I got to San Diego and started through my physicals and stuff out there they had for us, I flunked, got sent back. I was discharged from the Marine Corps. And so I came back in the spring of 1943. And my next-door neighbor who had been my roommate in NTAC [North Texas Agricultural College] had joined the air force under a new plan. They were taking in seventeen-year-olds, and when they got eighteen they would call them up for cadets. He had done that, and he was waiting to go into the air force. So I went up and talked to them and told them I had this medical discharge over my head. And they said, "Well, if you can pass our mental and you can pass our physical, and you say you can, I will get you into cadets." So I passed the mental. I went down to take the physical. I was flying high, and they hit me right in the face again: "You've got high blood pressure." So that kept me out of anything for over a year.

And I went back to school in a different way. I got a job at the war plant out in Arlington, or Grand Prairie, and they sent me back to school, night school, in Arlington. So I went back a semester of school in Arlington. I was supposed to have gone and left in September of 1943. And they didn't call me up, so I went to the head of the draft board. Being Lancaster, you know everybody and everybody knows you. And he said, "Melvin, why don't you just give up?" And I said, "Well, give me a chance anyway. I think I can pass the physical. I've been going to the doctors." So he more or less told me I might as well just give up.

And so I had taken a job with Dallas Power and Light, a day job. And while I was on this job, I read in the *Dallas Morning News*, in the want ads, I saw they were looking for ambulance drivers for immediate service overseas. And so [I] called the telephone number that afternoon and got an interview the next day with the person who put the ad in. . . . And he said, "Well, you're the type of people we're recruiting now. I think . . . you have a good shot of being offered a chance to go overseas."

I fooled around a couple of months. I didn't think we was ever going to go. I thought the war was going to be over before we even got in. [Eventually we were sent to Italy.] . . . But going overseas, it took us thirty days to get to Naples, Italy. . . . But I guess the most beautiful sight was going through the Straits of—I guess the Straits of Sicily, between Sicily and the boot. We went through one Sunday afternoon, and that was several hundred miles below Naples. Finally, the next day, which was a Monday, we landed in Naples. We pulled up to the dock, and we disembarked onto the side of a ship that had been sunk and was laying on its side, and that's what we got onto when we got off of our ship and went on ashore. And Naples had a big harbor and the city, kind of, built around it. . . . [W]e stayed one week in Naples.

• • •

After dinner [one] night somebody came in the front door. And it was chilly out there. They were all bundled up and all. And they took our commanding officer into a room off to the side. Then they were in there about thirty minutes, and then they came out. And I was just about ready to go to my ambulance to go to sleep, because I was leaving early the next morning. And our lieutenant said, "Well, we've got a problem here." He said, "They want ten volunteers to go with Company 567. And all we can say is that you'll be leaving Italy. And we need ten volunteers." There was

eleven people there, eleven people volunteered. He said, "Okay." We got down and—"We'll just take you by seniority." And so they turned to me and a friend of mine that came overseas together. They said, "You two are tied for the tenth place." And there was a deck of cards on the table. And our lieutenant said, "Why don't y'all draw cards to see who goes? High man goes." I turned a tre. The other guy turned a deuce. So I got to leave Italy.

And we went out on the other side of—just outside of Leghorn [Livorno, Italy]. And we left that night. We joined the 567 down the other side of the mountain. And then we went to— from Leghorn they took us by LST [landing ship, tank] over to France. And it was getting spring, and it was some beautiful flowers in the valley. We could see the snow-capped mountains off to our right over in Switzerland and southern part of France. It took us six days, I think it was, to get to Belgium. And then we went from there to southern Holland. We were there a few days. We had four platoons of about thirty-five ambulances each. All of a sudden, they said that we were going into Germany. And unknown to us we were going to Belsen concentration camp, Bergen-Belsen.

And the afternoon that we arrived at Belsen . . . Belsen is a town. Bergen I think is also a town. But we were in convoy, and all of a sudden, the convoy slowed down. And then— I was probably in the first half of the convoy. And as we came up to the end of the forest that we were in—we'd been in this forest for about twenty miles—and we looked over to our left, and there was a camp over there. And the gates were open on the camp. Then there was about a half a dozen or so men in striped uniforms just wandering around. I mean, it was like they were in a daze. I don't know how we— I don't know. I don't remember that we knew much about concentration camps and all or not.

But the gates were open and they were free to do what they wanted to do, and it just seemed like they were wandering around like zombies. And then we went on past the camp. And about a mile, a mile and a half north of the camp was a SS barracks. It had been a training—there had been a training facility there since, oh, about the middle thirties, I guess. There were dormitories built, two rows of them. And in the middle there were some wooden buildings, one-story buildings. The dormitories were about three, four stories high. They were the SS barracks, is what they were. I don't know whether it was built for a cavalry post or not, but it looked like that these little wooden, part-stone, one-story huts that were in the middle, between them, might have been a place for horses.

. . . The British had left 250 engineers there, or an engineering company. And the camp had been without food and water for a couple of weeks. They said from the time it was liberated until the time we got there, ten days to two weeks, they had lost sixty thousand people. When we got there, there was forty to fifty thousand left in the camp. It had started in 1939 as a prisoner-of-war camp for Russian prisoners, and then they had added the concentration camp onto it. It was probably one of the smallest concentration camps that they had. Covered less than fifty acres.

We went in—the first day we went into the camp, I went in as a stretcher-bearer. And the English had all kinds of protective gear on; we didn't. They'd just spray us [for decontamination], so we all were gray-headed there for a couple of months, spraying us. They'd spray us down the back of our neck and all. And we went in and there was a medical team. The doctors would, or a doctor would say which patient was too far gone, and we'd skip those. And we were in a women's section, and they would—the doctor had a couple of orderlies with him. They would strip off the clothing of a person and then wrap them in a blanket and put them on the stretcher. We'd carry them out, and we would help them get the women on the stretcher. And there was one woman just fighting us like everything. She thought that we were taking her to the crematorium, which they did. They took—sometimes when they went in to get the bodies and there were some that were not quite dead yet, they would pick them up and take them to the crematorium also, evidently.

There was, when we got there, there was six hundred a day dying in the camp, and at the end there it was down to a hundred a day. We would take them up to a—one of these little huts I was telling you about that ran between the barracks. And they would take them in there and strip their clothes off of them and de-lice them and cut their hair, and get the lice out of their hair and cut their hair, and scrub them real good and put new clothing on them. And then they would move them into the hospital section. And there at the last we had German nurses that were doing the first cleanup on the patients, and then they were moving them into . . . SS dormitories that had been turned into hospitals.

And so, anyway, in the camp it was dead bodies around. They had some Germans who were in a flatbed truck going around picking up bodies. We would pick up women. We would pick up a woman and beside her was a corpse. But—then you had to watch where you walked because there was filth everywhere. The engineers had got them some water by detouring the creek below the camp into the camp. They had latrines built by just digging a trench and putting boards over it and drilling holes in the thing. And it was all out in the open, and women would just go up and squat on the top of the hole. And there was dead— there was an open grave on our side that they were putting about a thousand to two thousand bodies in. We had to drive right by it going out. And they had Germans standing in the bottom of the pit stacking bodies. And I remember one time the—a lot of times people's eyes would be opened, and it looked like that they were staring at you. I don't know how many of those graves that they had. I think some of them might have even been up to four thousand in a grave.

Took about ten days for us to clear it out. The war ended while we were in the midst of our work, and we stayed on. The war ended about May the sixth or seventh. And I think it was May the—I thought it was May the twelfth or twenty-first that the camp burned. And the operation, I guess, had been over with quite—several days, and I was in the camp. And there probably wasn't a half a dozen people in the camp, I don't know. They were going here and there and everywhere. A lot of them had gone to Paris on leave. And I saw this black smoke going up into the sky. And some—I asked somebody, I said, "What in the world is going on?" And somebody said, "They're burning the camp, or what's left of it." So I jumped in the ambulance and drove down there. And, I mean, that was the blackest smoke I'd ever seen. . . . [I]t looked like the fires of hell.

RAYMOND STEWART WATSON

Excerpts from an interview conducted by Stephen M. Sloan

April 5, 2012

My college I went to, the first year was out at what they called the NTAC [North Texas Agricultural College] out at Arlington, which is now University of Texas–Arlington. But then I went on to A&M [Texas A&M University]. [I studied chemical engineering because], like most students, you know, you have some things you like to do, and [some things] you don't. And I decided that I didn't want to be on a drafting board for two or three years or four years, or whatever it was, after I got out of college. But I wanted engineering, so I picked an engineering course that I didn't think I'd be on a drafting board for a while. Now, that might be a strange reason for picking that, but that was at the time. But I was glad I did it.

[As] far as our military experience there, I was with the corps [Texas A&M Corps of Cadets]. And the first two years at A&M you had to be in military, but the last two years you had to sign a contract, you know, to be an officer, if you wanted to go ahead and continue in ROTC. So I did sign that, and in my junior year they pulled us out and I went to OCS [Officer Candidate School], since I didn't have my summer camp. And after OCS they sent me to Florida so we could practice landings and what have you.

And this was about the time they were thinking about going into France, so they sent me over there and sent me to Southampton. And I was at Southampton, but I didn't get called up for the landing. But I was there at Southampton when I did see many of the bodies coming back from—from what happened on the beach, from the D-Day invasion.

But then they sent me on—they sent me on up to—right—shortly after that. Well, I say, not shortly after D-Day, but it was in December of, I think it was '44, I guess, that they sent me over to join the Eighty-Seventh Chemical Mortar Battalion. And we shot smoke screens for when we crossed—in river crossings and so forth. . . .

• • •

It was [toward the end of the Bulge], which was when the US Army and the others beginning to—you know, got things pulled together where they was pushing back. It was. And when I first went over— You know, a lot of times you think you'll be getting instruction from various people, but not that. I mean, I had to go over, find my way over to somebody in Paris, and I got direction. And some unit I got—that I went to—they furnished a driver, and they said, "Well, it's up in Liege," or up in that part of the country, in Belgium. So we took out and I had a map, and just the driver and I. So we didn't have a whole lot of instructions on how to get there, where they were, and along the way I had to ask. Well, I knew the outfit that I was supposed to go with, but I didn't know where they were. So I had a little bit of a problem of finally finding out where they were. They were out in the woods, in the Ardennes Forest.

And that was—when I went in and reported to the colonel, that was quite an incident. He said, "I asked for a sergeant that I have, that has been through—since D-Day had been with me. And I asked for a battlefield commission for him. And they sent me you." He says, "You'll be out of here in two weeks, feetfirst." So that was my reception into the unit. But I did join the unit. And the unit commander was a Tennessean, and I had to wrestle him. I'll bet you we wrestled for two hours. I think after that they accepted me because it was a whole different story then. I became one of them.

Well, he said, "Let's fight," and so it was a wrestling match. Thank goodness he didn't get the best of it. [We] had the whole blooming platoon [watching us]. It was something, because, you know, over here the officers were separated from the enlisted men and so forth, but over there we were all together. I mean, we ate together, we had the same where we slept and so forth. It was the officers right along with the men. So, I mean, it was a lot different than what you'd be if it was on the stateside. They accepted me. I mean, most of them had, of course, had been there during—on D-Day and all the way through. And I came in. Of course, they thought I was a greenhorn. And I guess I was, to a certain extent, but I had been around mortars. . . . But anyway, they did accept me.

Well, we were in the forest, Ardennes Forest, and they shelled us. They shelled us quite a bit at the time. And the first thing I knew that a foxhole wasn't worth shooting at, because in the forest the artillery shell would hit the limbs and the stuff would fall right down, whether you was in a foxhole or not. But it—I think the—it was cold. We had more casualties from frozen feet than we had from people being shot. We had people being shot but, I mean, the most of our casualties were frozen feet. So you took care of your feet. And I learned that pretty quick. And I also learned not to go into a fire because, you know, you go in there and you get warmed up and so forth, and you come back and you've got to get used to cold all over again.

• • •

[We] weren't the outfit that went into Buchenwald. They were on our right. And we heard that they were placed there where there were—there was a camp, and there were just a lot of dead people. And we didn't—I didn't—we didn't know what the camp was at the time, but later on found out about it. But it was— They told me some stories about it, all the dead people and what have you, that I had to go over there because— Being a forward observer, we'd go up for two or three weeks, and then they'd be pulled back and let somebody go up again. And the time that I was back off the front line, I went over there to see what it was.

. . . [You] can see from some of the pictures we had that they stacked the bodies. They were just stacking up. They'd have them facing one direction on the first layer. The next layer, they'd turn them around forty-five degrees [sic; ninety degrees], and then they'd go up about five stacks high. And they were—I couldn't count how many people that were just—just dead. And every one of them were skin and bones. It was awful. I mean, the odor was bad and—well, you just didn't think a human could treat humans like that. But that was awful. I mean, anybody that saw that—it's something you don't ever want to see again. I mean, that many people just stacked up dead, and skin and bones to begin with.

[The camp had been liberated two or three days earlier.] Probably two days. It was—I mean, it traveled fast. Communications traveled fast that way, and whenever that happened, well, the—it could have been three days, but I think it was about two days after they took over. Now, all the German—that were—had something to do with it, they had gone, but there were a few Germans around. But then I know that later on the—one or two of the generals had the whole town come in and just go over that whole thing. And they made some of them crawl over all the bodies. I don't know whether that was revenge or what, but the whole thing was just something that you never want to see again.

There were still some [inmates wandering around]. There

were still some that had not been killed. But there wasn't too many, but there were still some, yes. In fact, also about that time was when we were beginning to see a lot of American prisoners that were released. And they came in, and they were hungry. And they—they were pitiful because they weren't treated too well. I know that we had to watch our stuff because they'd steal it. But I can understand that.

I went through [Buchenwald]. I went through it. They had a lot of steel doors and stuff. They didn't have the ovens like they had in some of the other camps, but they did kill. But of course, the barracks and all that sort of stuff, were just, you know, were really— They were awful. [They were preparing the bodies for burial.] . . . [T]hey had them stacked up, getting them ready for burial. But they didn't have a chance to do it. And I wasn't there when they brought the townspeople in, but I think that was an eye-opener for a lot of those Germans.

We didn't [receive] direct encouragement to visit the camp. I mean, I didn't see any direct—somebody from higher up come and do it, but we wanted to. Now, they might have encouraged some, I don't know. But our outfit—I just wanted to go over there. I'd heard about it, and I didn't believe it. But I did after I got there.

I didn't think . . . human beings could treat other human beings that way. I really didn't. But—well, it's hard to say. I think a lot of people either said, "Well, you know, it didn't happen," or—even Germans, or what have you. But I think it was—I don't know that just the basic people were much different than over here. I mean, a lot of them just didn't pay any attention to really what was happening. And I think I see that over here from time to time. But I think they got a real eye-opener.

• • •

I didn't want the army as a career, but if I needed to go back, I was ready to go back in Korea, and so forth, even though I had two daughters, what have you. But I felt that any situation like [the Holocaust], we need to do something.

The one thing I will say is, it did—we had some young people, and you know, some of them were—I don't know, I guess they were hardened, but they would go—they see a ring or something on a dead body, they'd just cut the finger off and do that. I mean, some of that happened with our people. And that's something I couldn't take. I mean, anytime I found out about it, I tried to do something about it. But that trait, I guess, is in a lot of people, maybe all of us.

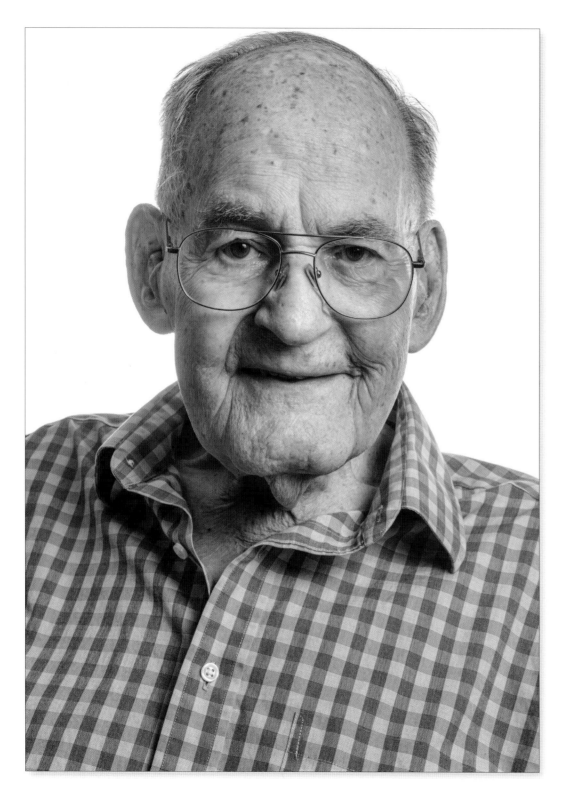

GEORGE H. WESSELS

Excerpts from an interview conducted by Stephen M. Sloan

March 2, 2012

Well, I was born out on the farm—actually a little town called Matlock [Iowa] that was not too far from where Sibley is. But I was born on the—out on the farm. The doctor came as far as he could with his car and then my father had to go get him with the bobsled because it was— And anyhow, I was three years old when they moved to Sibley. And then I grew up on the farm there and went to the eighth grade there. And then I had to help on the farm because my parents owned two farms up there, each 160 acres. So I never did go to high school.

And then in '44, when I turned eighteen, I registered for the draft. And went to Fort Dodge for a physical, and they asked if I wanted to be in the navy or the army. And I said, "The navy." So I took a navy physical. Then a couple months later they called me up. I go to Fort Snelling. And they told me—I said, "I'm supposed to be in the navy." They said, "Sorry, navy's full." He said, "You're in the army." And that was it. And then I was at Fort Snelling, I guess, for about a week, all told. And then they discovered that I was only about three months—eighteen years and three months old—so they couldn't put me in the infantry.

So they sent me to Camp Stewart, Georgia, for radar and searchlight and antiaircraft training.

We had infantry basic for half the day, and then we had the training for another half the day. But we had finished all of our radar training—I had gone through all of the infantry—the infiltration course twice, and the—fired all the weapons and everything. And we were all set to go out in the field for our two-week bivouac, and that would have completed our training. But they canceled the training and shipped our whole battery to Camp Robinson, Arkansas. And put us back to the, like, the sixth week of infantry basic. So I went through all of the stuff all over again. Went through the infiltration course twice again, fired all the weapons again.

. . . And one thing I remember also, I had a toothache, and then I had a decayed tooth. I went to the dentist at Camp Stewart, Georgia. He said, "That's going to have to come out," he said. So he put a shot in there, and he says, "Go sit out there for about fifteen or twenty minutes," he says, "and I'll call you back in." I walked out and sat down. And I hadn't sat down but—not even I think—I guess five minutes, and they called me back in. And he goes—I could hear it crack, you know. He said, "Does that hurt?"

I says, "Yes!" He says, "That's funny," he says. "It shouldn't." Wow, and he pulls it out. He crammed my mouth full of cotton and stopped the blood and sent me back to the barracks. And then that afternoon I had to go take a ten-mile hike. I still have that tooth missing over here.

• • •

[I hadn't traveled much before then.] I think the furthest I got was Sioux City, Iowa. It's the first time I rode on a train. And then—well, they put us on a troop train from Camp Stewart to Camp Robinson. So then after we finished basic at Camp Robinson, I got a ten-day leave to go home, and then I had to report out to Fort Meade, Maryland. This was about the first part of January of '45. I had the leave and then I went—reported out to Fort Meade. And then, at Fort Meade, they had us participate in a live-fire demonstration for the congressmen and stuff like that. They wanted to show them this new proximity fuse they had developed for the artillery, where they could put air bursts over the enemy artillery. So we did a mock assault—did a mock assault wave, and they fired that stuff out ahead of us.

And then, after that, why, a couple days later went to New York, and then got on the *Queen Elizabeth*. And it just took us six and half days to go across from New York Harbor to Glasgow, Scotland. We got off the train, got on the—I mean, got off the boat, got on the train, went to Southampton, on the coast—on the English Channel. Got off the train, walked on an LST [landing ship, tank], went across the channel. There were about four hundred of us crammed into the tank deck of that—at the bottom of this LST, and there was about two or three inches of this old greasy water.

And then we got across the channel and the—they didn't want to run all the way up and drop the ramp on the beach because all they had to do was, they have an anchor in the back of those things. They can drop the anchor and then run on up and then drag themselves back off with the anchor. But they were afraid they wouldn't be able to get back off. So they dumped us in about knee-deep water. Now, this is in winter. And the English Channel there. So we all got soaked up to about our knees, you know. Welcome to France.

We got to France there, and then we got on trucks and rode on trucks for a ways. And then we got on some of these old forty and eight boxcars and went from there to close to Belgium. And we got off and got back on trucks. . . . And then they drove us— They were sitting on the west bank of the Maas River, and the Germans were on the other side. And what had happened, the Germans had opened the spillways on the dams upstream, and then they blew up the mechanisms to close them. See, and then they caused the Maas River to flood, so it wound up being about a mile wide instead of just a quarter of a mile. When we got off the trucks at the Seventy-Fifth Division Headquarters, General Porter was the division commander. He welcomed us, and he said— he said, "Welcome to the Seventy-Fifth Infantry Division." He says, "You may have heard about R&R, and all that stuff," he says, "but forget it!" He says, "We're going to attack, attack, attack until this is all over." That's exactly what he did, but, of course, we didn't get started for about ten days.

. . . [F]inally we got across the Maas River. And I don't remember too much between it and the Rhine. And I know, we were moving all the time, all the time, all the time. And so it only took us about, I guess, ten days from the Maas River to get up to the Rhine River, because it was my birthday on the tenth. And we'd dug in on top of the dyke, my assistant BAR [Browning automatic rifle] man and myself. It was just an outpost up on top of the dyke there during the— We just manned it during the night, because otherwise, they could observe and they could see you. But for the rest of the time there, we'd—we were back behind the dyke in a farmhouse.

• • •

We started out on the thirty-first of March. And we finally—the division finally got the clearance to, you know, start using the bridge. And then—but we—yeah, we started our first attack on the thirty-first of March, there across the river. And that was the same day when—actually, when we ran into those slave labor camps, and that other battalion took that synthetic rubber plant.

We were advancing up the road in column actually, and, you know, with your fifteen—five-yard interval between you. And we were just moving on up, and then these buildings off to the side there, kind of like a stockade. But evidently the Germans had taken off. And then the prisoners inside there had broken—I guess they broke down the gate or whatever. They were already coming out, and they were all over the place. But as we went by—we couldn't stop there. Our squad leader said, "Don't stop. Don't mingle. Don't stop." So we kept going. And, oh, a couple of them grabbed my hand, kissed my hand. And then after that, I stuck my hand up under my BAR sling so they couldn't get a hold of it. Because they were all covered with scabies and—well, we thought they were scabies, but I guess what they were, were sores from malnutrition.

But they looked horrible. And they were emaciated, skinny. I had never seen, you know, all the time— I came from Iowa. I had never seen anybody that thin. And we saw a few yellow stars for the Jews on them, but there weren't very many. And they—we didn't even know actually at that time what it meant. We thought they were, like, trustees, or something like that, for the prison camp.

[We hadn't heard of the camps.] Not before then. We didn't even know it when we went along there and that—you know, it was a slave labor camp. We didn't know. They told us later on, about three to four days later. They said, "Oh, that was a slave labor camp that we went in."

[The survivors] were very happy to see us, yeah. There were big smiles on their faces.

WILLIAM A. WOMACK

Excerpts from an interview conducted by Stephen M. Sloan

May 18, 2012

I grew up there in east Fort Worth. And in—about '38—I was about seventeen, I imagine—yeah, seventeen. I was going to— There weren't any jobs around for kids, so I joined the Texas National Guard just to get their twenty-one dollars a month. And in '39, well, actually in 1940, they started mobilizing the National Guard, and they were drafting twenty-year-olds. I was going to be nineteen in October, so I'd be prime draft bait in about a year. I'd already been in the guard for about a year and a half, so I just went ahead and joined up with them. And we went to Camp Bowie, Texas, down at Brownwood; stayed there about a year, training. And we were supposed to get out in a year. I was actually home, waiting on a discharge, on December 7, 1941. And, of course, you know what happened then.

So I just—I went back to the camp and they said, "No discharges. Everybody's in for the duration." In '42, we got—the whole division got transferred to north Florida, when we was taking amphibious training. And this unit I was in was the Texas National Guard Thirty-Sixth Infantry Division. After about a year there, we went on maneuvers up in the Pinelands of North Carolina, South Carolina, for several months. Then we moved

on up to Cape Cod, a camp called Camp Edwards, which is when we were taking amphibious training out in Nantucket Bay. That was in 1942. In the spring, I think it was April or May of '43, we loaded on this ship, and the whole division went to North Africa.

And that wasn't bad over there, the combat. Where we landed was a little place called Mers-el-Kébir, which wasn't very far from Oran. And we stayed there at Mostaganem, I think, for about a month, and we moved to the west coast, to the Casablanca area. And we practiced our surveying. That's where I learned to run a survey instrument and how to "lay the battery," we called it. And we were in combat reserves because the Afrika Korps was just about defeated at that time. And our whole divisions caught one German in about a four-month period. And then, let's see, we got up there in April, and then in August, the same year, we went to—made the Salerno invasion in Italy.

•••

I remember the worst casualty I encountered was there in Italy. We were in a position, and there was a creek behind us, a little circular creek. We were in a direct observation of that Monte Cassino Abbey. We were in that position probably twenty-eight or thirty days. All we got was small-arms fire—I mean mortar fire—in our position. One day they decided they'd really give us a working-over and they did. I was in the dugout up in front of the battery. The battery was firing over me. So we started getting the fire, and when we shut down, everybody went in their holes. I was listening over the radio when the number one gun hollered, "Help, help, we got casualties on number one." I said, "Stand by, I'll call the medics." I called the medics on another phone. And in just a minute an ambulance went right by us and down to the gun position, but the shelling continued. Then we got another phone call. This guy said, "God damn, both our medics are down." I said, "Well, I'll be down there."

So I threw the phone down and took off, jumped out of my hole and run down there. Shells were still coming in. They'd come in, and there was a big bank to my left, sort of an erosional feature, and it went down into the creek. I was running down parallel to that bank. Shells were hitting up in that bank, and every time I'd hear one coming in I'd hit the ground and double up. I lost my helmet, so I didn't pick it up. I didn't go back and pick it up. I finally got down there to where the ambulance was, and it was shot all to pieces. Two medics, they said. One of them was hit in the back, and he couldn't move. He was a captain, and he was laying down close to that bank on one of the wheels of the ambulance. And the driver was laying under the ambulance. I looked around, and there were three or four bodies lying in the creek, floating in the creek. So I waded out about waist-deep and got one, drug him back and turned him over. He started talking, you know. I went back and got another one, turned him over, and he started moving. I knew he was—and this last one I got, he just kind of moved a little bit. And in the meantime, another guy from the other gun came over and helped me. So there was two of us out there in that creek.

When we got all those guys out, two of them were dead. We left the two dead ones laying there. And I got in the ambulance, and one of the shells had hit up on that bank, and a big fragment of the shell had went right through the right window, through the instrumental panel, right in front of the—through the steering wheel. I said, "This thing will never start." But I turned on the switch and hit the starter. Cranked right up. I drove out to

Highway 6, turned left, and saw a little sign on the road that said Aid Station Point, with an arrow. We went down there, drove in there. The captain come out—somebody come out and said, "I'll take those two right there." I said, "What about the other four?" He said, "I don't have any more room for them. Take them down to that other ambulance, that other field hospital." I said, "Where is that?" He said, "About two miles down the road." So I took them down there and I unloaded them, and all of those guys survived. I was sitting in there muddy, dirty. I didn't have my hat. I picked it up when we went by. I said, "You got a cup of coffee?" And they gave me a cup of coffee, and I sit there drinking this coffee. I looked up, and then in walks my best buddy with a big old bandage around his arm. I said, "God, what happened to you?" He said, "I was lighting a fire to make some coffee and it caught my shirt on fire." So that was one of the hazardous experiences I had.

• • •

We didn't have too much . . . trouble until—I can't think—we really—well, except when we started capturing those concentration camps. The only one I went to was Landsberg, and I didn't know about that until they come up. Well, the captain come down and said, "I want you to take three men from this gun section and get on this truck and go up to this—follow this other truck." I said, "Okay, what are we going to do?" He said, "There's something up there you need to see." So that's when we saw Landsberg. It was a—kind of a pretty location, really. There was a big row of dense pine—fir trees and a lot of them scattered around.

When we got there, all the prisoners were on the inside. We went inside, and then the prisoners started, kind of, drifting out. Then we saw all these dead folks, and then we decided we'd get out of there. The poor inmates were just kind of—were in sort of a daze. They didn't act like they knew what they were doing. They just milling around from one place to the other, in between the trucks. And they'd get in the trucks and out of the trucks. Some of them were just boys, you know, like teenagers. And some of them were old men. But they all walked with sort of a stiff-legged gait. They were nothing but bones. They just had a little skin. So they wanted—they'd come up and they'd say, "Food, food." Of course, when we first started that, we had rations in the truck and food scattered around the area, you know, like soldiers do. They'd get so much every day and they wouldn't eat it all, so we started giving them stuff. And the next day we found out we made a big mistake in doing that, because our rations were so concentrated that it killed some of them. Why, they had been on a diet of water and turnips for years, and they didn't—couldn't handle any high-protein food.

. . . The fence looked like it was prefabricated. The posts were . . . about a four-by-four, and they'd stick it up this way, and then a two-by-four out this way on another post and then a two-by-four on the ground so that they were self-sustaining. You didn't have to dig a hole to put them in, but they were supported by barbed wire. They had a mesh wire on this side, but heavy barbed wire on the top. They were just out on sort of a flat plain. Looked like they had cleared the trees off, because the trees were in a perfect line. Looked like they'd just took a bulldozer and went down that and cleared all the trees off. And there were a few trees around the front, but the gates were made out of wood and wire, real flimsy. But they had guard towers, probably fourteen, fifteen feet high. There was a wall—the fences were about, I'd say, probably eight feet, eight to nine feet, about like these walls here. But the guard towers were about twice that high, and some of them were—had insulators on them, were electrified. But these that were in Landsberg that I saw, weren't. They were just tacked on there with a staple, looked like you would use them around the barnyard. Barbed wire was very different, definitely. It had spikes on it that long. And these houses, barracks, I guess, some of them were sort of buried. One of them we saw. But most of them were just sitting out there in plain— I didn't go in. I wasn't about to go in any of those things. But they'd have windows down, and it wasn't—just ordinary small buildings. They were about ten to twelve feet apart. But I don't know about where the— I imagine they had separate latrines somewhere, bathrooms. But then I didn't look around that closely. I saw all those dead bodies, and I wanted to get out of there.

They wanted us to see the atrocities that were committed.

And these—most of the bodies were just bones and skins. They were starved to death, I think. The cold will kill you. But that was just one of the things they wanted us to see about why we were there, why we were fighting. But it was something I haven't forgotten easily.

LEE H. BERG

Excerpts from an interview conducted by Ronnie Morgan

May 2, 1994

I had made a summer trip with a friend of mine as a work away to Europe for two and a half months. My parents gave me two hundred dollars and his parents gave him two hundred dollars and when we got to London, we jumped ship and we traveled Europe. And we did that for about two and a half months. That was back in 1934–35, somewhere in there. I was very young. Like a merchant marine—a cotton ship.

I got back to the United States and landed in Jacksonville, Florida, and I called my father and told him that I was going to stay in the merchant marines and I was going to make a ten-month trip to the Far East. I was seventeen, eighteen then, and he said, "Well, Mother and I'd like to see you before you do that." And I said, "Well, I'm going to New Orleans. The boat is going to New Orleans. And you can pick us up in New Orleans." Well, when I got to New Orleans, my father was there in his car and he put me in his car and drove me to Gulf Coast Military Academy. And that's where I went instead of going to the Far East.

. . . [It was 1934 when we jumped ship in Europe] and we had no idea [what was going on there then]. . . . We jumped ship in London and we got our way to the coast of England, hitchhiking.

And then we got a ferry boat that took us across the channel. And when we got across the channel, we bought old beat-up bicycles and we bicycled our way to Paris. . . . We didn't have backpacks in those days. In those days, we had old, beat-up bicycles. We just had what we were wearing. And we basically lived off the land. We did have [the] two hundred dollars, and that took us a long way, and then when we got to Paris, we went to Belgium, and from Belgium off to Holland. On our bicycles. . . . Then when we got up to Holland, we turned ourselves in to the immigration people and they said they'd been looking all over Europe for us and they put us back on the same ship that we came over on and they sent us back to the United States.

. . . I went to military school and graduated. Then went to University of Illinois, went there for two years, came home, went to work, and that's where I picked up and joined the Thirty-Sixth Division and went into the service, and that's when the war started a year later.

• • •

From the Elbe River, this is the area of when we went south and got into the concentration camp of Dachau outside of Munich.

Well, we were sent down to try to assist in the— You can imagine the chaos that we ran into walking into this camp. . . . The thing that is so distinct is the smell. . . . You can't imagine. And the bodies. (*Cries gently. Overwhelmed.*)

[We were one of the first troops in Dachau.] And there was a— (*Breaks down from the memory.*) It's hard to describe how you can walk into a situation like that. I mean it's just, you just walk in and you really and truly can't imagine what has happened. No. . . . I mean you had heard that these atrocities were going on but you're young, you're—you're fighting a war, but when you actually walk in and you see it and you smell it, it's just unbelievable.

Well, I saw, I saw people without clothes on. Dead. Stacked up. The odor was just, you can't imagine human beings living or being treated that way. I mean, it's hard to visualize how anybody, anybody, I mean you possibly think that beasts live like that, but it's utterly impossible in your mind to think that one human being would do that to another human being. I mean it's just something that you— I don't know how to explain it.

Well, all I can remember is that I went up this road and I saw this tremendous fenced-in area, buildings inside of it, but the odor. I mean, I think the odor is what made me sicker than anything else. I mean I saw the bodies. Of course, I had seen bodies in war or that had been decaying and all of that, but I had never, I had never smelled anything like that before. And it just seemed to get into your taste and everything. I looked around me and I said, "My God, how can you treat people this way? Or why do you treat people this way? I mean, you don't treat animals like this." Sure, sure, I knew who they were—[Jewish people]. But at the time, I don't know. . . . I think that was my first realization what this war was all about.

And that was the way they were treating the people. And it was just, I couldn't— It's just hard to describe, how they— And at that point in time, I remember, I went back there at camp that night or a couple days or two or three days, I don't remember, time had just— I know I couldn't eat. I don't think I ate anything for weeks. Every time I saw food, I got nauseated. And I think that's when I wrote the rabbi a letter.

. . . We knew we were going into a concentration camp. But we didn't know exactly, I didn't know that it was going to be this type of a camp. We were just told, I was just told, "Lieutenant, take these troops. You're going into a concentration camp." And then what we had to do was to create some kind of order. Everything was havoc. Get these people, bodies buried, properly sorted out, and just assist every way that we possibly could.

I don't remember any conversations with any of them. . . .

But me being the only Jewish officer, I think it possibly affected me more than it did anybody else. Or I felt it did. Maybe. Maybe at this point in time in my life, I think I grew up at this point. I think up to that time I'd been very— But when I saw that, it ages you. It ages you mentally and physically.

. . . [Before I'd walked into the camps, I'd heard stories about atrocities.] You can imagine, twenty-five, twenty-six years old, fighting a war, you'd hear about these things. But you said to yourself, "Well, did this really happen?" And then all of a sudden (*slaps hands together*), you see it. And you know it's happened. . . . [I'd heard they were doing this to the Jews.] Oh, sure. Oh, certainly. And then you knew it was there. Because you were seeing it. You couldn't help from not knowing it was there. You saw the people with the marks on them. And you knew that it was a concentration camp.

• • •

. . . There were some German civilians left at the camp. Sure were. And you hated them. You hated them. But you know— In other words, you can make excuses for them, but it was just like anybody else. You know, they were given instructions. If they didn't do it, they would've gotten killed. I mean, that's basically the only attitude that you could take, that they were carrying out instructions from up above.

I was there maybe a week. [I went back every day. We cleaned the camp up.] . . . I knew nothing about any of the other camps. I only knew about Dachau.

We were mostly disposing of the bodies and burying the bodies and trying to get out some of the filth that was in the camp. And that took a considerable amount of time, even after we left, I'm sure.

I have no idea [how many bodies I buried]. Of course, a lot of them were already buried, in ditches. There was a tremendous job of trying to determine who, what, when, and where. At that point in time, they had . . . very little identification.

. . . We had heard some of the people say how these people had been hauled in and came in on boxcars, and women were thrown into one group and men thrown into another. The thing that really disturbed me, I think as much as anything else, was the mistreatment of the women. Just, they were just absolutely treated terrible. I mean, stripped of all their clothing, humiliated. Just, the way they described it, it's just hard to believe. That human beings would do anything like that. . . .

[I saw them on the other side of the fence. Skinny.] No food. And of course, the main thing we tried to do with the ones that were still alive was to get them out and get them someplace and to get them protected. Put clothing on them.

[I was told this was a camp where they brought Jews.] We were told we were going to Dachau to liberate a Jewish concentration camp. Yes.

I remember the women and the men. Older men too.

My attitude, I think, after that was completely changed. I think that I aged. I think that aged me. I think that up until that time, I don't think I really was a man. When I saw that, I said, "This war can't go on like this. This is unbelievable."

• • •

[I wrote to my rabbi] within the first two or three days. I didn't remember writing this letter until . . . [my friend] brought to my attention a copy of the letter . . . [the rabbi] had written to me.

This letter was dated in May of 1945. [It is] from Rabbi David Lefkowitz of Temple Emanu-El in Dallas.

> I can well understand the effect that German brutality visited upon the Jewish people has had on you. Of course every Jew feels the same, but I wonder whether the Jews will remember and the world in general will not forget? They are showing pictures of the horrors of the concentration camps here in the United States, but even these views may not bring home to some people, perhaps to many people, the lessons that underlie the whole horrible story. Namely that we must guard against all outbursts of racial and reli-

> gious hatred and must conserve religion against that kind of paganism that made these horrors possible. I see you are working in a displaced persons camp. That must be a pretty sad place. Be as gentle and as thoughtful to those people as you possibly can. They have suffered much.

• • •

This has been the first time in my life that I have ever discussed this with anybody as much as I have with you. But I think it's important that I did.

WILSON CANAFAX

Excerpts from an interview conducted by Stephen M. Sloan

September 14, 2011

I was born in the town of Millsap [Texas]. My father was the station agent for the railroad that went through Millsap at that time. My mother became ill, and Dad moved the family. And I was the last of four children, three of whom were living. Dad moved to Dallas to get my mother near medical help, and—but she died. And so I was brought up in the city of Dallas. And Dad had a hard time. He had— His work was seven days a week. Ironically, he had no way of transportation, so he walked three miles to and three miles from his work every day. So you add that up over thirty-five years, and you'll see how much he walked. And he never weighed over 125 pounds. Walked all of his weight off.

But my grandmother—our grandmother was the one who came into the home to look after us and see that we had clean clothes. And if we had patched clothes, they were still clean. And she got us off to school every day. In fact, the last six years of my public school education, I didn't miss a class, nor was I tardy. That's impossible today, but I did it, and I was glad I could. I got special recognition for it, and that was okay.

I graduated from high school at Woodrow Wilson High in Dallas. And I heard there was a school in Fort Worth where you could get a job and go to school. So I came over and I found a job

working. And my grandmother, who had brought me up, had no place to go, so I took her with me to college. And we literally stayed there together for four years in an apartment. She looked after my food, my clothing, and everything else, and made me ready for school every day, like she had been when I was in high school. And I finished Texas Wesleyan. I came to SMU [Southern Methodist University] Seminary in Dallas. And I was just an average student. I was a pretty good guy, but an average student.

. . . Mine was no big to-do. That is, I didn't see a streak of lightning across the sky that tells you to go preach. Mine was sort of a gradual feeling. I just got into it because that was what I wanted to do. And I felt like I had a personal relationship with God to respond to the work that I was called to do. And so it was a genuine feeling, a genuine call, and I appreciate so much the fact that I could be in the ministry and serve in such varied ways. . . .

And the war was going on, and they were needing chaplains. And so I guess out of patriotism or whatever, I told them I'd be ready to go if they could use me. And they said yes. That's when the army took me in as a chaplain. I was sent to Fort Devins, Massachusetts, for training. And it was not a lengthy training, but it was there—I was there during the wintertime, and it gets cold in the interior Massachusetts, I can tell you. Texas light-blood going up there and it was cold. And I was given assignment from there to the parachute school at Fort Benning, Georgia. And I appreciated that. I was working with men who were under risk, but I was not a jumper. I was getting ready to be, and they said, "We need you more elsewhere." So they picked me up and sent me to Europe. And I stayed in a depot in Belgium a few weeks—I think three weeks—near the little town of Dolhain.

They assigned me to the 1110th Engineer Combat Group, which was up in the middle part of Germany. And that's where I met my group. They received me with genuine appreciation and friendship. So I was there when the war ended; I was at Marburg. And having been over there such a brief time, they said, "We want you to stay and do some chaplaincy work." So they sent me down to Stuttgart. And I was at Stuttgart for a while. From Stuttgart, I was sent up to Frankfurt, headquarters chaplain. I enjoyed that. The bigwigs were there, and I had a chance to be of service to them. There I was a young chaplain, a chaplain still green behind the ears trying to be a chaplain to those four-star people.

• • •

The outfit I was with was the 1110th Engineer Combat Group. And we had moved up to Eisenach in that period of transition. And while I was at Eisenach—we were there about thirty days, I guess—I had heard that there was a death camp. We didn't know much about concentration camps, or death camps, and neither did the German people. You've often heard it said that the German leadership kept these camps quiet as they could, away from people, and they did a pretty good job of it. Some of the German people I got to know quite well after the war I'm convinced were not fully aware of what those camps were. I heard there was one close by to Eisenach. So I decided I'd go nearby, about fifteen miles away, to this place they called a death camp, or a concentration camp. And I didn't know much what to find. It was strictly an informal visit.

There was a room about—not quite as big as this room. The ceilings were higher. But this room had pegs in it about where the ceiling is in this room. Those pegs were about six or eight feet apart. They were heavy pegs. There were little stools around. They would bring the German people in there, and put them on those stools, and put ropes around their necks, and have them

there, maybe—I didn't count the number of places there were—but I guess at one time maybe they could exterminate forty or fifty people. Kick those stools out from underneath them. I've never tried to myself imagine what it looked like to see all those people struggling and trying to live. I didn't see it, but my imagination was there. That was the killing room. They would take them over to ovens on one side of the room and put the bodies in there and exterminate them. They did away with them there. This is where they killed people. It's where they burned their bodies.

My conversations at Buchenwald were rather limited. There were no formal tours going through, and they didn't try to organize people to bring them in and let them see it. I was dealing with men, looking at them, almost 100 percent of whom could not speak English. And they were looking at me, and I was a chaplain, a man of God. What could I do for them? And there wasn't much I could do. I still carry that feeling of inadequacy. When I was there with them and had been presented with a situation that my faith said, "Okay, here you are now. What can you do, and what are you doing with it?" And so I felt like I couldn't do much with it. And did I depend on the grace of God? Yes. God's grace was present then, even though I couldn't feel it the way I should, it was there, and it's been with me ever since that time.

The first thing I thought about was—the first thing that came in was one of guilt. Now, you've had the kind of faith which you have told yourself will hold up to anything. You have the kind of expression to yourself with the idea that you can face anything. Okay, old boy, you have faced something you can't handle, now what are you going to do? Well, it was a spiritual struggle. . . . I didn't want to come to you or anybody else and say, "You know, my faith isn't strong enough to bear this." I was guilty, I felt guilt. And the feeling at that time was, I didn't have the faith I should have, but yet I did. And went through it, came out of it, and have continued. And I still have, I don't say flashbacks, but I go back to that time of, "Why couldn't you handle it?" The main thing that I could do is to get back home and get to work. Deal with people, prepare sermons, preach them. Just be a part of what you were meant to be to begin with.

•••

A person wearing captain's bars could go most anyplace, and chaplains were given commissions. And so I thought, "Well, I'll go down and see about this place." And my jeep driver and I drove down there. And we parked near the front entrance, you know, started over toward the front. And before I got to the front entrance, there was a young fellow, came up to me speaking perfect English. Looked like he was about fifteen or sixteen years old. He was too young to have been in the German army. And he said, "I see you have a cross on your lapel. Are you a chaplain?" I said, "Yes." He said, "Could you—do you think you could do us a favor?" I said, "Well, I can try." It turned out that this person that was talking to me was the young fellow, Eliezer Wiesel, Eliezer Wiesel, who's known better today as Elie Wiesel. There have been documentaries on his life. Well, he didn't know me from Adam, and same thing. I just knew I was meeting a young fellow. And I was six or eight years older than he, and he was too young to go into the German army, and I was—I was too young to really be a chaplain, but I was there anyhow.

And he says, "Could you do something for us?" And I said, "Well, I'll do my best if I can help you." And he said, "First of all, I'd like to take you through some parts of the camp here." And I didn't know what that meant because I didn't go there for any formal take-through. I went through the main entrance, I remember that well, and walked in. And as you've heard the expression *dead men walking*, that's the way the—the—I don't like to use the word *inmate*. I don't like to use the word *residents*. That's where the people who were in the concentration camp looked. I went to several of them, some who could speak English, and I could talk a little bit with them. I planned a worship service for them. A chaplain had many different ways to put things together, so I planned a Jewish worship service for those in the Buchenwald death camp who wanted to come.

So many of them had wanted nothing to do with religion, but those who were genuine in their faith enjoyed the opportunity to come to a worship service; they came. . . . I remember the first time. We got our carry-alls, those big trucks, and put the people who could be carried in those things to a place where we could

have a worship service. They had to be lifted on. They had to be carried on, crying. They never thought they'd be alive. Many of them had been there, not knowing too much about their past, because they'd always been under some kind of incarceration—concentration. But we got them in the carry-alls and took them to the place of worship. And I was in charge of the worship service.

We had some little prayer books that were distributed among those that wanted them. And on one side of it was Hebrew, Hebrew prayers. Other side was English. So as they went through the service in Hebrew, then I could follow along in English itself. They cried. They shouted. When they got through, they were just raising hands, sort of like our Pentecostals today raise theirs. They were just raising their hands in joy and appreciation. They didn't think they'd ever see that again. They didn't think they'd be alive.

WILLIAM E. DANNER, SR.
Excerpts from an interview conducted by Stephen M. Sloan

March 6, 2013

One of the first things I can basically remember was my grand-dad. I can remember seeing this white-haired old gentleman sitting back in his wicker rocker. And I would come in, and he would call me Southpaw or Tarheel. And that was my granddad. And he passed away in 1928. So I must have been about five years old at the time. I was born and raised within that area in central Indiana. We lived on farms at some times and lived in the city. I graduated from Elwood High School in 1941. Elwood was the home of [Republican presidential candidate] Wendell Willkie. And he caused me and a couple of others to get kicked out of history class a couple of times because the teacher we had lived in Willkie's home. And he was a hot Democrat, and we was always razzing him about it.

My father worked several things. He was the hired hand. But we had a great life on the farm. And I learned to be a farmer. And I thought when I graduated from high school that that's what I would be, because in high school, I majored in vocational agriculture. I took all the agriculture courses, but sometime in my senior year, I decided that was not it, that I wanted to go to college. I was raised as a Baptist and Franklin College is a Baptist school, and that's where I wanted to go to school. I was accepted, and I started there in the fall of 1942. And I did not get a semester completed before I was drafted. I dropped out of school, was drafted, went into the army, and when I got out of the army, I went back to Franklin in January of '46.

I came from a military background. My eighth-generation great-grandfather had come from Germany in 1725, sometime in about that time. They left Germany for religious oppression. He had four sons. Three of them were in the American Revolutionary War. The one that our family is derived from is referred to in the genealogy as the revolutionary soldier. My great-granddad was in the Civil War. He died later as a result from a wound that he received at the Battle of Chickamauga. My dad had a brother that died, that was killed a month before the armistice in Germany, in France in World War I. Of course, I was drafted. And I had two uncles that were draftees. Well, the one was called from the National Guard, and my dad's youngest brother was a draftee in World War II. As far as I know, everybody just went back to what they were doing before.

I started college in the fall of '42, Franklin College at Franklin, Indiana, and was drafted in February of '43. The army had a specialized—Army Specialized Training Program. They were going to teach us to be graduate engineers in eighteen months. And I was there when the invasion took place, and they sent us all back to the army. I took my basic training at Camp Swift, Texas, in the artillery as a forward observer. I was a radio operator for forward artillery. After the ASTP, I was sent back to the army, and I went to the antitank company, 414th Infantry Regiment of the 104th Infantry Division.

I knew that I would be drafted. I would get a draft card. We all had to register. I knew that I would be called. Of course, it was 1943 before I was drafted. I left Indiana. Was drafted at Fort Benjamin Harrison—inducted at Fort Benjamin Harrison in Indianapolis. We left there on, ironically, the fifth day of March, 1943. It was five degrees below zero. We had on our wool uniforms, our wool underwear, the whole works. Three days later, we landed at Camp Swift, Texas. It was eighty-five degrees. And there we were, still in winter clothes.

When we went in, we were given intelligence-type exams. We were going through all kinds. And I think that's where they got the information. . . . I was given orders to go. Everybody—a lot of the people that went into ASTP—were out of the air force, United States Army Air Corps at the time. And they had— A lot of them were sergeants and the like, but everybody was reduced to a PFC [private first class]. And I went to Louisiana State University, and we lived in the rooms underneath the stadium. But when the invasion happened, we were all sent back to the army.

I was assigned to the 104th Infantry Division. They had just finished their maneuvers from Camp Adair, Oregon, down to Yuma, Arizona. We met in some place in the desert outside of Yuma, and we were there just a short period of time. We were in a tent camp out there. We loaded on board trains, and we went to Camp Carson, Colorado, where we finished our training to smooth out the rough spots. And in August of 1944, we left Camp Carson for Europe. I was with a regimental antitank company. We had 57-millimeter antitank guns, and our crew was thoroughly trained. Everybody within the squad was trained for every position on that gun. I guess we were lucky. When we got to Europe, we were lucky enough to never encounter a Tiger tank.

We shipped out of New York. We landed in Cherbourg, France, on the seventh day of September, ninety-one days after the invasion. We were the first division to land directly on the continent from the States. We were not in France too long. We made a couple of different moves in there. I remember I voted in my first presidential election from a foxhole in France in 1944.

But then we moved up into Belgium and Holland. And one little town, we were outside, I think, a day or two before we actually got into combat. We went into this Belgian town, and there was a movie. And we went, three or four of us went to the movie. When we came out of the movie, there was one little old lady there. Came up to us, and she invited us to her house for dinner. We gratefully accepted and asked her if there was anything that we could do. And she says, well, her husband was an invalid and they had trouble getting milk. So the next— That night, I got into the mess tent. I midnight-requisitioned a gallon can of milk, and we took it the next day. And there were about four Canadian soldiers there also that she had invited, and they had taken Spam. And she had spaghetti and meatballs that was made with Spam, and it was good. And I don't know how many pies that lady had baked, but she would bring you— After we finished the meal, she would bring a big piece of pie. And by the time you had finished it, and you couldn't say no, she had another piece sitting down there in front of you. But it was just, the people were so grateful at that time that they would almost do anything.

• • •

We approached the Nordhausen camp. I know somebody come back and said, "They've found a concentration camp. They've taken it." And we went up to see what was going on. And there was bodies. A building there that had stairwells, and there were bodies stacked under the stairwell like cordwood. They were laying out in the streets. And the medics come up. They brought up a medical battalion because some of them were still alive. Some of them were so weak that just a weak, warm broth did them in. They were that far gone to start with. And the people of Nordhausen, they denied knowing it was going on. But they found out in a hurry. They came out and had to clear up all the bodies. All the male residents of the city of Nordhausen, they had them out picking up bodies. But we were there just a couple of days after that. Then we moved on, and that was—

But I still cannot realize why people deny the fact that it took place. I know it did. I took—I—I saw it. We had other places where we got into towns or places where they had this slave labor. They were— And the people we saw, some were Russian, Polish, all nationalities of people that were just slave laborers for the German forces. This was just a factory. And these people were just worked, worked to death.

I guess we'd heard of them, but we came upon this unexpectedly. They found it. And there were two of them, Nordhausen and Dora, the two concentration camps that the 104th was involved in liberating. And it's a horrible picture to see. You just can't realize the physical damage that was done. And I think, most of these people that died in these camps like Nordhausen, I think, they were all buried in a common grave. Where they would bring in a bulldozer and dig a grave, and the bodies were all placed in there with no—nothing done. Just, I guess, to cover them up, to get them out, and keep the disease and whatever, any kind of something spreading is just—sanitary reasons as much as anything.

In the battlefields, I think, bodies were cleared up. The GIs, both sides—and fact is, there's times that they called truces over there so that wounded and the like could be cleared off of a battlefield. I know this had happened. But there, there was nothing. These people, I don't know who stacked them. Whether they had the people that were the slave laborers to clean out the bodies and stack them up like that or lay them out in the streets, but they were laid like a parking lot, just rows and rows of bodies. But there was still a few that were alive.

• • •

They had an event over here at the synagogue and they had all the veterans that were there stand up. And we were sitting way in the back. And the other noises, I didn't quite understand. Genie poked me in the ribs and says, "Stand up. Stand up." So I did. And there at the end, the lady that was the emcee of the program, she says, "We are honored to have a liberator in our midst today." And she started through the biography that they had on this memorial that they had out at Fort Bliss. And Genie again was poking me in the ribs and telling me to "Stand up. Stand up." And I stood up for myself then. It was— People appreciate it. At least

to me, it showed their appreciation, the Jewish community itself, they appreciated it. And the ones that were really involved in the Holocaust, the two ladies here, they appreciated somebody that knew what happened, that could tell what happened.

WILLIAM DIPPO

Excerpts from an interview conducted by Stephen M. Sloan

October 21, 2011

I'll start with date of birth—the real date of birth—okay, June 15, 1925. That was a good year for grapes, I was told later on. Boy, we'll go from there—hey, wait a minute, me at a loss for words? (*laughs*) I have two sisters, both junior to me. My dad was born in 1900. And he wanted to enlist in the army during World War I, but his mother, my grandmother, was a tough old Irish lady. Killfoyle was her last name, and she boxed his ears a few times, and he realized he couldn't enlist. So when my war came, I had nobody to box my ears. I could do just about what I wanted, if it was not immoral or illegal. And I live by that credo to this day. Mom was a stay-at-home mom. And there's not much to say. She had raised three children. And—oh, she did hit me with a coat hanger when I told her I enlisted in the army. That was in November 1942.

Knowing that I couldn't get in at seventeen, I had a couple of friends who made counterfeit coupons like the ones you had to have to buy sugar, gasoline, et cetera. They were counterfeiting those. So who do I go to fix my birth certificate? My two friends, who subsequently were in jail while I was in Bastogne. So anyway, I got in at seventeen. I enlisted, so I asked for the cavalry. I

was a pretty good horse rider, as a matter of fact. I could jump. I could curry the tail. I was used to that because of the National Guard. I used to go away with my dad, who was in the National Guard. . . . And I would go when I was, like, thirteen—twelve, thirteen, fourteen—I would go away to summer camp when they were called to active duty for two weeks. And that's where I learned how to take care of a horse. When they weren't looking, I used to ride them bareback around in the corral. So anyway, I enlisted for the cavalry.

. . . I didn't know any better. There was no cavalry. . . . When I went down to enlist, I went with my buddy. I can't remember his name really. He was a buddy all right, but I just— It's been so many, sixty some-odd years, I can't remember. And he didn't go to my school or my church, so I never knew him that well. And he had one of these elbows like Senator McCain has, but [McCain's] was from being a prisoner. . . . [My buddy] was born this way, you know. So I said, "Okay, I'll go navy." So we went down together. The navy took him, arm or no arm, but wouldn't take me. I couldn't see the wall, and I was too skinny. Too tall to be that skinny. He was skinny, but he was short. So I didn't bother to ask in the marines, and the army air force, I'm sure, wouldn't have taken me. But somebody stuck their head out of the door as

I was going down the hall from the post office to go home. And I was feeling a little upset and unhappy that they wouldn't take me.

And then I heard, "Psst, psst." I turned around and there was this big fellow, with all sorts of stripes on his arm and medals. And he says, "Come here, son." So I went in. I told him, I said, "Okay, I want to enlist in the cavalry." "Okay. Are you eighteen?" Well, I got ahead of myself there on that eighteen thing. I says, "Yes, I'll bring in my birth certificate." He says, "You do that. So in the meantime, you eat a whole bunch of bananas, and we'll give you glasses. Don't worry about that." "And the cavalry?" "And the cavalry." So anyway, my grandfather was a policeman, and I told him exactly what I did. And he was all for it. In fact, he was in the Spanish-American War, but he never got out of Florida. Never got to Cuba, but he was there. He was a veteran of the Spanish-American War, so . . . I thought I'd uphold the name.

. . . Six-foot-one, and I weighed—well, I don't weigh that much. I do, a little more, but not much. And the navy didn't want me in there, like I said. But bananas, I weighed 138, so what the hell? I didn't put lead in my pockets or anything. I knew they'd take me. So anyway, Mom was okay on that, and Dad finally came around. Of course, Grandpa was pushing me in, because he's got a lot of stories from other policemen about me. But nothing was ever—I never was booked, as it were, because, "Oh, Dippo." "Yes." "Oh, Officer Dippo, Frank?" "Yeah, that's my grandpa." "Okay, go ahead." I'd have a shirt full of apples or pears or something. That kind of nonsense as kids would do, I guess.

• • •

Our mission that particular day that we took off was to liberate Mauthausen concentration camp. Prior to our leaving, a day before, I'll back up, on the sixth of May the Eleventh Armored Division, Combat Command A cavalry, armored cavalry, got there first. And I didn't think—I was of the opinion there wasn't anybody there, any Germans there. Well, in uniform anyway, or armed. That's the way I was told, anyway. But the war still hadn't ended, but the cavalry sent out help—asking for medical help immediately. And, of course, the purification would be our job, which we didn't get until the next day, on the seventh of May.

Seventh of May we, the rest of the Combat Command A, arrived at Mauthausen concentration camp. And what we beheld—what we saw—and I'm sure I speak for my comrades—was worse, the condition of the people and what had transpired prior to our arrival was worse than the battlefield. They were terrible. They were covered with sores. They weighed seventy pounds. They were—if they were alive at all, they didn't go over seventy pounds. And they were all sick and had lice, and—and it was terrible. But the medicals got in there that afternoon in force. They set up a tent to triage, but they didn't have to triage. Everybody was the same, practically. But they took care of the women and children first. And they gave them first aid and gave them shots and operated on them and sent them back—further back into a more stationed hospital—a station hospital, a MASH [mobile army surgical hospital] unit, more or less. And then, from there, they could go on, if they were still alive.

. . . [T]he scene that we beheld when we went in to Mauthausen was really the living dead. And it doesn't get to you as badly as it does when you see a human walking like he's dead. . . . [T]o see these human beings walking, shuffling, and mumbling, and they don't know what to do, and what's going on. They—they—it was terrible. It was pretty hard to take for most of us. That's it.

But we did—the engineers—we dug. We had a trench dug by our dozers. And I recall, it was at least fifteen yards long and over six feet deep and at least five yards wide. And all the bodies had been stacked already, mostly on flatbeds, but some on the ground. And our commanders, our military commanders—military government commanders—made it known to the *bürgermeister* of the adjoining village that they were to show up at such-and-such a time.

And so the government—a colonel from the military government people—ordered the *bürgermeister* of that little village . . . to attend the burial of the deceased. And they were to wear their finest clothes. And no gloves. And they were to take each skeleton, each body down into the hole. Boy, you could hear them, "We didn't know. We didn't know." . . . But we all know they knew. Then the burial. We had a chaplain from every religion say—after our dozers covered them. It was our dozers that covered them over. Then . . . the commanding general had all the chaplains of all the faiths that was represented in our division. It couldn't—I'm sure there weren't any religions that weren't represented here. . . . The Torah was read from. And all, everybody, all the chaplains and the people of the city—town, had to stay right with us. And believe it or not, some of them knelt while this was going on. Because Europe, if you go way back, before the other religions came, was always the Catholic religion. And they were kneeling, and crying, and moaning that they didn't know.

The stench of the ovens would have—should have given it away, but it was—didn't even need that. It was obvious what was going on in that enclosed area, Mauthausen. It would go down in infamy as man's worst inhumanity to man.

• • •

[I]f I mention it or even think about it, I get emotional. It's— I can't help it. Because it's there, it'll never go away. But—and then you see it in the museums, and you see it on television even. Well, you don't get a close look, but I have seen Mauthausen on television as well. But now it's all dolled up, and, of course, they can't go back and show those pictures on television, of course. But it is something that should never, never, never happen again. I don't care what we have to do to stop it. I'd be the first to go if they'd take me.

SIGMUND LIBERMAN

Excerpts from an interview conducted by Stephen M. Sloan

December 14, 2011

Well, I was born and raised in Seattle, Washington. And my mother was born in Ceylon, India. Her father was an English— followed the English army as a tailor. She came to San Francisco at six years old. And she was lost during the earthquake [ca. 1906], and they found her. And then they moved to Seattle. My father came over from Poland at ten years old and went to San Francisco with—to meet his uncle. And then he went to Seattle, and then went to Alaska before World War I. And he came out to enlist in the army. And he was not drafted, but he did not serve. He was—[had] something wrong with him.

And I was just raised there as a normal kid. I went to Garfield High School. I was the editor of our high school paper and went on to college. I wanted to become a journalist at that time, but my father said, "No, you're going to be an engineer or doctor or lawyer, one of the professions." And so I ran away from home and went to Alaska after one year of college, because I could not afford it. And he wouldn't contribute to my college other than the fields that he wanted.

I went to Alaska and worked for the US Army Engineers [US Army Corps of Engineers] for two years. And we were building a navy base at Seward, Alaska, on December 7. And the Japanese did fly over Seward. People don't know that, but they did fly over. And I was very friendly with the commander of the base that we were building. I was assistant to the superintendent and, as a result, he asked me to join the navy. So I came out to join the navy air force. And I was color-blind at that time, so they wouldn't take me. So I enlisted in the army. And I came to Texas— Weatherford, Texas—as an infantry trainee. And then the infantry sent me to Fordham University as an engineering cadet for a year under the AST Program [ASTP, or Army Specialized Training Program]. And I was at Fordham and the army recalled all those students, and we all went to Camp Carson, Colorado, and joined the 104th Timberwolves.

. . .

[Being of Polish descent, my father watched the events in Europe.] . . . His sister was left there with two children. And her husband and the family were on a train going to Dachau. And the father pushed her and the two kids off the train when they were traveling through France. And so she lived with the French people during the war. And he was—went to concentration camp and was cremated. But we finally found her in Antwerp, Belgium. And so my father and I paid her way and sent her to Israel, and she died in Israel. But her daughter came to New York and worked for a French railroad. And her son stayed in Israel and became a major in the tank force during the war.

• • •

The same guy in a foxhole with you. And when somebody got shot who was close to you, it really worried you. And my men, a couple of times when we were surrounded by Germans, we were in a warehouse filled with turnips. And knowing that I was Jewish, my comrades put us in this big pile of turnips, covered us up so we wouldn't be captured, and three or four of them surrendered and were sent to a POW camp. And it was a good thing the Germans didn't shoot into the turnips. They came in with their bayonets and poked in, but we were further in than they were. So that was one of my scariest positions and one that showed real camaraderie with my fellow soldiers.

I mean, they were with me, you might say, because of close camaraderieship of all of us. And we were really pretty close together. And one time our jeep driver, who was a Mexican from Nogales, Arizona, came and brought food to us through the enemy lines, because we were stranded. And so everybody knew what each other stood for. And I guess being Jewish, they respected me. And being in the infantry and not back in quartermaster or something, they had respect for me even greater.

[We'd] heard on the news [about the Nazi strategy toward the Jewish people] and everything. And the *Stars and Stripes* would have stories. We knew about it, but I didn't know we were going to go to a concentration camp where you would get close to it. Nordhausen was a confinement camp for workers. Nobody was shot or killed—was shot. They all starved to death. They were Polish and French and Russian workers that worked on the V-2 bomb at Nordhausen. And the Germans in the city said they couldn't know—they didn't know anything about that camp. Yet you could smell the stench of the dead people seven, eight miles away.

[Our] troops—the 104th was assigned to the city of Nordhausen. And they heard about this concentration camp, so they sent me out there because I could speak a little German, and I could speak Yiddish a little bit. So I understood. And they sent me to the camp to help them, whatever was necessary. And we tried to get all our aid people in there to give those aids to those that were still alive. But as I showed you in the pictures, they were stacked up dead all over the place. And the living were like skeletons. But in the city of Nordhausen, our troops, not me, but our 104th Infantry Division, caught a German convoy, a train filled with Jews. They were leaving because they knew we were there. And they were leaving them to go to another camp, and go to a crematorium, or kill them or something. But at Nordhausen, all the people starved to death. And it was strange to see them, you know, nothing but bones and skin. And those living were barely walking around. And I remember seeing some of them, and they were French. And none of them—there weren't any Jews at that time in the camp because they were migrating out.

And in the town, Nordhausen, there was all—I went in there to get all the men with shovels to come back to the camp and dig the graves for the dead. And they thought that I was going to have them come in and dig their own grave, and we would shoot them. But it turned out the other way. And we made them carry all of the bodies around to another hill, on the other side, and make them go through town, so the people knew that there was a concentration camp out there. [*They had to carry the bodies through town] to get to this hill on the other side. Yeah, I know another serviceman said that they—in that town, they had forbid the citizens to wear gloves while they did it. They had to do it with their bare hands.*]

• • •

When somebody dies it comes back to me. And when this holocaust is going on now, in Africa and Syria and those places, I get memories of that picker thing because it's just back here again, even though we didn't want to see it happen again. But in Africa and in the Near East, it's going on again today. And we had hoped when we freed those camps and we got rid of Hitler and freed Germany that we'd never see that again. But—

[What does being a liberator mean to me?] Well, I think that it meant that we did something well, and accomplished a certain role. And not all of the Jews in Europe were cremated, there were some saved. There are Holocaust victims left here in the States, and also in the city here. [Being Jewish], I think it made a difference because I was part of them. And I had ancestors from there. And I had ancestors killed during the—and I don't know how many others—than my father's brother-in-law. I don't know how many other people were killed. I'm grateful that I had participated in it. And I'll always remember that I was part of it. And I was on the good part. And I just hope that I could do something about these things that are going on now, but it's almost impossible at my age and in my condition to do anything about that, even though I'd like to. But, who knows? And I think that the main thing is that we should not forget. And that's the one thing that I've been talking about at high schools and different schools. Most kids today don't even remember World War II. And here was the annihilation of a complete race of people. And they're trying to do it again, as I said, in Africa. Well, it just is impossible to think of it happening, even in Africa or the Near East, where somebody, like in Syria, can kill a thousand people, or in Africa, hundreds of thousands. It doesn't seem possible in their minds that they could do this, but here it is.

• • •

[You] would never expect to see the things that we saw going through there, I mean, where the dead were just stacked up. And I had been seeing dead people before, and people got shot, but here they were just lying, and nothing but skin and bones. And they'd been lying there maybe for weeks, or even months. And—I don't know, it's something—a sight that I'll never forget. It's implanted in my mind. And every time I look at those pictures, I could almost cry. And now the only good thing is I gave a speech one time, to a high school here in Dallas, about the Holocaust and Nordhausen. And a girl came up to me after the speech and said, "Thank you, Mr. Liberman." I said, "Thank me for what?" "For you liberating the camp. You—" she said, "I wouldn't be here now, if you hadn't done that. My grandfather was there."

So here it brought back—again, one of the men that we freed went on to have grandchildren here in Dallas, Texas. So that—

you know, it makes you real sad. And of course, it was sixty-five years ago, but still, the memory of it is—is rough.

BEN LOVE

Excerpts from an interview conducted by Lydia Osadechey and Ronnie Morgan

January 8, 1993

[B]efore going to Austin, Texas, to begin my studies there at the University of Texas . . . I had been educated in Paris, but the Paris to which I refer in this instance was Paris, Texas, not Paris, France. I was in the University of Texas; the Japanese had bombed Pearl Harbor December the seventh. I graduated from law school in 1941, and the war at that moment seemed remote, although the newspapers, the radios—this is before television—would announce day after that in Europe, . . . Hitler was on the roll, he had nothing but successes. We would read about the Stuka dive bombers before killing so many civilians.

And then in the Pacific, the Japanese—again, just success after success.

I think at that time we didn't envision that we were going to lose the war, but we knew that this was not going to be an easy thing. And even at seventeen, which I was in 1941, we inwardly began to recognize that our time would come. It was not going to be short—of short duration. When I turned eighteen, I had already decided either to volunteer for the navy submarine force or for the Army Air Corps, and I volunteered for both on the day that I turned eighteen. . . . The Army Air Corps contacted me

first, and having passed all the physicals and what other exams that they gave, I went in the Army Air Corps in February of 1942 and began my training in short order. I was eighteen. Most of the men who . . . became cadets, Army Air Corps cadets, training to perform some responsibility in flying were eighteen, nineteen, twenty, and a few twenty-one, but we were young.

I got my commission in April of '44, my wings in April of '44, and was assigned to a crew in B-17 Flying Fortresses, and in short order, after another month's training with my first crew, we were on board what had been a Swedish luxury liner, on our way to Great Britain as a part of the Eighth Air Force. We landed at Liverpool and in a few hours took a train to a place that all of us were unfamiliar with. It was the 351st Bomb Group that was for—B-17 Flying Fortress Group, and that was in Polebrook, near Peterborough in East Anglia, England.

We were, remember, very young, and we had all volunteered and had a sense of adventure, melded and blended with the realization that it was pretty serious business.

• • •

[T]he enemy was Hitler. Hitler personified the German nation, and the overrunning of weaker people was embalmed in our minds. There was no question as to whether or not we had a purpose—ever. We had seen pictures of the concentration camps, we had seen pictures of the slaughter in Warsaw, and that was part of our training. Not in a propaganda sense. I didn't hear the word "propaganda," I think, until about 1944. But what it was all about was pretty clear in our minds.

We were not— I do not want to turn this into a seemingly kind of adventure story. It wasn't Tom Swift, Buck Rogers kind of attitude that we had, but despite our youth, we felt that we were professionals, and that if Hitler continued and if Hitler had not been challenged and met squarely, that the world was in for a terrible chapter. We were—we were inspired—and I use that word here almost fifty years later—by Franklin Delano Roosevelt and by Winston Churchill, and in my case in particular, by the courage of Charles de Gaulle.

. . . There was no what you would call a propaganda movie or exhortation. It was simply a realistic identification of the slaughter that Hitler had launched against anyone who stood in his way. . . . I think there was a purity, a patriotism at that point in time among people of my generation, that we have seen at other points in time in this country's history. But the purity of patriotism was [different] from that which we saw in Vietnam and some other conflicts. And that's with no disparity on those brave guys that were in Vietnam. The difference was that this was universal, and during the Vietnam period, it was not universal.

• • •

[T]he reason I remained in Polebrook, I had the job of training younger crews, and so I was doing that from February 28 on; had been doing it in between missions, too. We'd take them up on practice bombing missions and bomb a place off the West Coast of Wales called Scares Rock. It was a great big rock that stuck up there out of the ocean. So they'd use that as our practice bombing and we could see our practice bombs hit, and grade the crews and so forth. But the war was over on May the eighth. And on May 10 we had orders from the Eighth Air Force. Our first orders were on a standby, because we did not know that . . . the Russians were going to stop at the line which had been designated, and we were told to stand by in combat readiness state, because if they

did not stop, we did not know what orders might come to make them abide by the agreement.

They did stop, and on May 10 we got orders from the Eighth Air Force to fly into Lenz, Austria, not with our combat crew but just our standard lead crew, and pick up the French officers who had been captured six years earlier in 1939 when the Maginot Line fell to the Germans; the Maginot Line being the great fortification that the French had built anticipating that it would repel any line into perpetuity, and as you may recall, Hitler with his Panzer divisions flanked it and it fell rapidly.

So we flew into Lenz, Austria, and very readily found the camp, prisoner-of-war camp, where the French officers were, and it was rather uneventful, other than just their happiness, their joy that they had survived the war, and here they were going to be flown back to their homeland and see their families for the first time in all these years, and so they were very, very happy. They were in good shape; they were healthy and their uniforms were clean. They were frayed worn, but they were in, you know, they were in fairly good condition, and it was a leisurely kind of thing.

. . . And one of the officers who could speak excellent English got me aside and said, "Captain, if you want to see what this was all about . . . you want to walk over the other side of this air field." And I walked over. He said there was a concentration camp there, but I didn't know the name of it, I didn't know anything else about it. And so I walked over. I can't recall today whether he walked over with me, showed me where it was, but anyway, I know I got there, and the sight I saw is very—very difficult for me to recount unemotionally, even all these years later.

There were human skeletons holding on the wire fence, I guess it was the electrified wire—obviously it wasn't at that moment—and men, women, children, some too weak to stand, had on their prison garb, identify by number, you know, just looking at them. They were just—you just can't imagine how man, civilized man—and presumably the Germans were civilized— how they could have inflicted that cruelty here in this century on people who had never harmed them, innocent people. And then I recall going back into some buildings that were the gas chambers and learned later that they, the Germans, had gassed two hundred thousand people there at Mauthausen.

I knew that [the prisoners] were those of the Jewish faith.

[When I entered the camp], there were three to five hundred [of them]. The advance medical units had not gotten there and so that compounded the horror, because the poor people there had not received medical attention yet. There was no German that I saw when I walked around—not every bit of it, but enough of it; as much as I could.

You would understand it better . . . if you weighed sixty-five pounds, and if you had on something that appeared to be made, as we used to call it in East Texas, a burlap bag or even a tote sack—rough, coarse material—and identified by a number, and just terrible conditions.

I did not [speak to them]. I mean, they— I only know what nationality they were, but they—I tried, but they couldn't understand me, and they were so weak and helpless that you wouldn't want to pull the last ounce of strength straining for them to understand, you know, what you were saying. I think they understood that we were from the United States Air Corps, and— [They were] too weak [to react to us]. They were just so weak that many of them [were] just lying there on the ground.

Someone had told us that the US medical teams were coming and that I recall the issue of food that we had brought coming up and we were told not to do it, that they had been deprived of food so long. If they were given food, they might become violently ill and as weak as they were . . .

It gave me confirmation of the faith that I placed in the leadership of our country; that Roosevelt was justified, that he knew that we had to eliminate Hitler and all that were associated with him.

• • •

[T]he sight—as a I say, it's a nightmare, and I'll never forget the sight. . . . We have learned that there were six million Jews who were killed. I can't imagine anything in this country that could have happened without there being an uprising of the people in Beaumont, Texas, if there had been that kind of camp on the outskirts of Beaumont, and—or anyplace else here in this nation.

It has carried forward throughout that length of time. I have great empathy for those who are in the minority segment. I don't care whether it's color, religion, whatever—great empathy. I am delighted and I have never said this before and maybe I haven't thought it out . . . but I hope I practice what I preach.

• • •

I have told my children and grandchildren [about my experiences at Mauthausen]. They don't understand it exactly. It's impossible for them to conceive, impossible for my children to understand, too, but that's the reason [this] work is important, I think.

I mean, you've got pictures—but maybe for children something like this might make an impact. . . . The discrimination of Mauthausen—loading people in cattle cars—for absolutely no reason, no inquiry as to what the law is, much less trying to follow it.

It's just because you've got the boot and the club and because someone has caused you to lose any individual thinking ability, you do the goose step and you take innocent people because someone who is mad himself, literally mad, tells you to do it, and you herd them into cattle cars and you take them to a Mauthausen.

. . . We have a lot to pass on, but that's one of the profound philosophical moral issues that we've got to pass along. We are passing on a lot of science, but that my being here today is I believe in what you believe in . . . that we mustn't forget, we mustn't forsake. We must graphically point out within the realm of our experience what a lack of tolerance can lead to.

JERRY B. MORGAN

Excerpts from an interview conducted by Stephen M. Sloan

May 18, 2012

I went to Oklahoma University after I graduated from high school. Mother went with us down there, rented a large home, and set up a dormitory for students. That year was a good one, successful. But, in the next summer, I went back to Oklahoma, back to Enid to work. Then, on her way back one night, she and the lady that helped her in her housekeeping ran into the back of a wagon, horse-drawn, in the middle of the night. She was killed. Well, I was determined—since my dad was so insistent on my getting an education—I was so determined that I went back to school for the next year.

But during that summer, I went to Camp— Let's see, we went from Barkeley—not Barkeley, but from Abilene to Louisiana for summer maneuvers. Those were serious maneuvers in preparation of what was to be induction into the army. On the way back home, we were told that we were going to let these guys out that didn't want to go, but the rest of us would be inducted in November. So we went into the service on November 4, 1940. So then, we went into Camp Barkeley from there. Camp Barkeley was built as a new camp at Abilene, Texas. I was sent with an advance party to Abilene to locate housing and everything for the unit. So when we got down there, it was being filled with recruits and new enlistments. It was kind of a confused thing, but it was more physical training than anything else.

One little incident that happened was that we had what was called a flotilla of the ships, and they were in command of a commodore. I don't know what a commodore's responsibility was, but he was the fleet commander. We sailed from Martha's Vineyard. We went out to an island to practice landing. The command came over the loudspeaker, "Now hear this." He said, "There will be a sound, a horn sound, and the gates will open on the front, and I want these vehicles off of here immediately." So we approached the island, the ship hit the sand, the horn sounded, the doors opened, and my first tank went off. But all that was showing after he departed from the ship was a machine gun above the water. We had hit a small reef. . . . The good part of it was that a couple of years later in Europe, I got a letter from the quartermaster—no, from ordnance—telling me that I owed eighty thousand dollars for that tank. I took the letter to my commanding officer, and I said, "Sir, what am I to do with this? I don't have the money and don't have the means." He said, "Well, let me take care of it." He tore it into small bits. That's the last we heard from it.

We went aboard a—the vehicles were transported on LSTs

The Texas Liberators   80

[landing ship, tanks], but the troops, our troops were on a cargo ship—well, actually a luxury Swedish liner which had been converted for army use. We landed at Mers-el-Kébir, Africa. We got a little bit of training there, but then, from there, we went to—well, I've forgotten the name of the port where we departed—but from there, we went to Italy, Salerno. . . . [F]rom there we went on north to various places: Benevento, Caserta. We got to the Volturno River where everything quieted down across the river from Monte Cassino. We were stagnated there. They withdrew us back to Naples to load to go to Anzio, and that was a new experience. We got aboard and got ashore safely, no problems whatsoever. Then, our corps commander decided that we were going to hold the little land that we had acquired. Well, Anzio was surrounded by mountains on the north and to the northeast. It gave the Germans time to set up a defense against us. So we sat there until May being shot and returned some shooting.

I spent 515 days in combat, and the worst I ever got hurt was on Anzio. I had become a company commander by that time. And I had driven one of my tanks through the back side, or the shore side, of a two-story building, a farmhouse, putting me inside the building to where he [the gunner] could shoot out the window during the day, if needed, and could come out and maneuver at nighttime. We had an aircraft that came over almost at an appointed time every night, and he would drop what were called butterfly bombs. It was a case that contained small parachute-equipped bombs that would detonate as they hit the ground. It was an antipersonnel thing. Well, I could hear the aircraft coming, and I knew I better get into cover. Well, one of— It was nighttime and dark, and I ran for the front door to go into the building, and someone had left a gasoline can on the steps. I hit it with my shin. But that was the worst that I was ever hurt during the war.

• • •

Well, the next day I knew was going to be different. We had heard all kinds of rumors about concentration camps, about how they treated people and what they did to them. One of the rumors that I remember was that they made lampshades out of human skin. Well, that sounded kind of far-fetched. But anyway, the next day

we were good to go from Nuremburg to Dachau and to come into Dachau from the northeast. And my approach unit was with the 158th Infantry. I borrowed—from my reconnaissance company, I borrowed an M8 [armored car, with a driver], got in it, and started south on that road. I got to the main east-west road that would lead me into Dachau. The objective was the camp, but there was a little community called Dachau. So I kept thinking, maybe we could get into, approach Dachau from the south. Our feeling was at this point that the German army was pretty much in disarray, and that they had decided that they were being beaten pretty badly. We really didn't anticipate much opposition, so I wasn't too afraid of wandering off by myself. So we got into the city of Dachau. It was a small town, but I noticed this one beautiful mansion there, about a three-story building. And I thought, "Well, that's the *bürgermeister's* house."

Anyway, there was a camp entry—I went on past that a little bit—and there was a railroad that was headed north-northeast. Dachau camp was just a—oh, less than a half a mile from the town of Dachau. So I told the driver to get on the railroad track and let's see where it would take us. It took us into Dachau. As we were going in on the railroad track, here is the main road, the main entrance into the camp from the town of Dachau. A tree-lined road. I didn't want to go in that way because I knew that if there was any resistance, it would be there, along there. So we just kept inching our way into town—or into the camp—and where it took us was to the ovens that were a part of the camp. It was well paved on both sides of the track, and the ovens were well built. And there were three gondola cars there. Well, we couldn't see—from where we were, we couldn't see into them. So I had the driver drive up alongside one of them. We both got out and got up on the deck of the M8 and looked in. *Believe me, the Holocaust existed.* They were loaded with bodies. The bodies still had their uniforms on, but they were purposely put there for putting into the ovens. The whole truth became evident at that time.

So I said, "Come on. Let's go move into camp and see what we can see." So we went—we drove along this well-paved street, I guess about, oh, maybe three hundred yards. We came to the first fence. It was about a ten-foot fence. Behind it were, as I recall, about five men in [striped] uniform. But they were kind of mute. They weren't exuberant or fearful or anything. They were just—you know, just had an indifferent feeling. There were no German soldiers in evidence anywhere. I think that because of Dachau being—I mean the previous day's battle—I think they had all evacuated. I was surprised at the low number of people that were in the quarters behind these buildings. Or that we saw. To the left were some barracks-like buildings. This idea of skins on lamps was in my mind. And I thought, "Let's go see what we might see." So I went into one of the buildings and the first thing I came to was an office. It was very well furnished, neat. There was, of course, no one there. But I didn't know—but what maybe later in the camps there might be some other people. I knew that I had no business being there. There wasn't anything I could do for those people.

So we turned around and went back out the main gate to the city of Dachau. And it was there that I—I knew we weren't going any farther than that because other units had liberated Munich, which was just down the road a bit. Munich would be the next objective, and we wouldn't be a part of it. So when I went out, I stopped at this big house I was talking about. Sure enough, it was the *bürgermeister's* house. His wife was there; he wasn't there, his wife was there. I had an interpreter, and I asked her where her husband was. She didn't know. And I said, "Well, okay. You have two hours to pack whatever you want to take with you and turn the house over to us. We're going to use it for a command post." It was no objection, no lamentation, no nothing. We went back about three hours later, and the house was vacant. Beautiful place. We stayed there about three days until we were given further orders.

. . . I didn't really know what to expect in the camp. And of course, we couldn't communicate with any of the prisoners because we couldn't speak the language. I had an interesting meeting with a fellow here in Midland about, oh, it was back in the spring. I went to a symphony concert and behind me was a Church of Christ minister that I vaguely knew. He introduced me to his guest who was a German Church of Christ minister who lived in that area. We had a little short discussion about Dachau. I told him that I had been there. He made the comment that most people assumed that that was a Jewish camp. He said yes, there were some Jews there, but the main part, the main use of that camp was for crime—people that committed major crimes—and for political prisoners. They were all treated the same, which was finally execution. It wasn't principally for Jewish people.

. . . I began to think about, well, why—how long had those people been in there? They couldn't have been in there over twenty-four hours. Otherwise, they would have begun to spoil. They were still in their clothing. So our timing there was such that, oh my God, panic set in, and they took off. This was what they were doing at the time they took off.

But *this was evidence* that there was a Holocaust.

JOHN "JACK" FERGUSON REYNOLDS

Excerpts from an interview conducted by Stephen M. Sloan

September 13, 2011

[I was at Texas A&M University] [p]robably half a semester. I still call myself a member of that class. [I left for] Fort Sam Houston. And from there, I was sent to Camp Claiborne, Louisiana. At Camp Claiborne I became a member of the 398th Engineer Regiment General Service, which was just being formed. And everybody in it, except a very small cadre of noncoms, was rookies, including the officers. And that was kind of interesting. Since I had a little bit of ROTC, both high school and A&M, and Boy Scouts, they made me a corporal. I knew how to set up a pup tent.

. . . [M]y basic was at Camp Claiborne. Halfway through that, they sent us to Arkansas, to work on a flood. We learned to build all kinds of stuff, you know, bridges and stuff like that. Gin poles and sheer legs and tripods and all kinds of stuff for moving equipment. But up in Arkansas, they were working on a flood of the White River. And so we learned how to match our slopes and to control seepage, how to build chimneys around sand boils so they wouldn't wash the levee out. We built a few bridges and then went back to, went back to Claiborne and finished up. And just before they finished up, they came and asked me if I wanted to go to the ASTP. And I said, "Well, what's that?" And they said, "We don't know." But it was the Army Specialized Training Program, and nobody knew what it was. So anyway, they sent me back to college, and I went first to LSU [Louisiana State University], which they called a STAR Unit, which was some kind of an acronym, I think, but only—it was just for casuals. And then they sent me up to Lake Forest College, on—it was thirty miles north of Chicago, on Lake Michigan, and—my training, well, it was about—it was kind of like a pre-engineering, but it wasn't as much as I'd had at A&M, you know. I had some liberal arts stuff in there too, geography and all. But anyway, that was— I started, I think, in September of '43, somewhere along in there. And along about in March of '44, well, they broke us up and sent us out to the California desert. And that's where we joined the 104th Infantry Division. And at that time there— An infantry division has about fourteen, fifteen thousand men in it. And they brought in five thousand replacements from the ASTP into the 104th. They were coming off of desert maneuvers at the time. And then they took us from there up to Camp Carson, Colorado, and we trained up there under General Terry Allen. And we specialized in night fighting. And then from there they sent us overseas.

Oh, I think everybody was in a pretty good mood [when we

crossed]. They did a little zigzagging, but I think the U-boat threat was mostly taken care of by that time. And there was always some guys playing cards or running a shell game, something like that. But the last— I do remember, though, that they handed out some little bitty books that were stapled together, little booklet deals. And some guy was teaching us a few words of French, how to pronounce it and—you know, "Where's the railroad station?" and all that kind of stuff was in this little book. And so we kind of went in for that. Then that little book, which I have since lost, when we got over there—when we finally got to where there were some people to try to talk to, was in Belgium. And it was in a Flemish part of Belgium, so the French equivalents didn't do much good. We were writing down little—I was—writing down little Flemish equivalents, and then we didn't stay in Belgium very long. Got over into Holland, so I was writing little Dutch equivalents in it. Writing very small, of course. And then I got into Germany, and for a long time there wasn't anybody to talk to, but when we did find somebody, well, we were writing German equivalents down. So all of my lexicon of German and French and Flemish and Dutch, it's lost.

[I had never been overseas before.] . . . [I]t was—damp. It was cold and damp. And this was in September and October. But in the Cotentin Peninsula—you know, that's where I'm really speaking of. Other places weren't that much different in climate. But it was—it was interesting. In one of the places where we were in Belgium, we was on the grounds of the Peter Paul Rubens home, Flemish painter. And, of course, that was where our headquarters was.

And a translator came by and said, "Now, we're not supposed to go to Brussels. It's been reserved for the British. So you're not supposed to go there. It's off-limits. And the train station is right over there." So we went off-limits that evening in Brussels. I remember, I think they gave us a couple of dollars or something—a very, very little bit of money. We didn't normally pay, but they gave us a little money. See, of course, we were making combat pay by now. But we decided we wanted something to eat, and we saw a sign on this door for a restaurant. We went in, went up the stairs, went down the hall, into the hall. Man comes to the door. He's dressed up in a white tie and tails. And all these ladies and gentlemen wearing their dining [formal wear]—you know.

He told us he didn't think we'd be comfortable in there. And I'm sure we wouldn't have. We couldn't have afforded a cup of coffee.

[Morale stayed pretty high.] . . . I could see those guys after they'd been fighting for a long time, though, and they got the thousand-yard stare. You know, just exhausted, that sort of thing. But—after this little foray into the Harz Mountains, we—I think we were lost. It wouldn't have been unusual with that particular officer. We went to a town called Duderstadt and spent the night in Duderstadt. And we met a couple of guys. One of them was from the 106th Infantry Division, which had been wiped out practically in the Bulge, and so he'd been a prisoner. They'd marched him east, and then they marched him back to the west. They get too close to the front on either side, and then they started him back east again. And this guy told them he was sick. And they didn't shoot him. They left him behind. So he was there when we got there.

Another little guy was a Jewish guy, I think. He wasn't in our—wasn't a soldier, and he was—the soldier hadn't had anything to eat. And I went in a bakery. And they had one loaf of bread, and I made them give it to me. I've thought since that I should have given half back to them, but I didn't then. We had plenty of food, but it wasn't with—our kitchen hadn't gotten there and—you know. So I wanted to feed the guy a little bit. He was starving. And so, anyway, this Jewish guy, he said, "Well, I can tell you where we can get eggs." So the next morning, before dawn, we started out. And we went out in the country for a few miles, and he went up, and I stayed with the vehicle. He went up and rapped on the window, woke the people up, came back with a hundred eggs. And so we took them back to town and were feeding this guy that was starving. He would say, "Well, I'm going to be sick. I'm going to be sick." He'd go ahead and eat it anyway.

And then, the following day was when we went—reached Nordhausen.

[I had never heard of it.] Zero. Never heard of it. We pulled into Nordhausen in the afternoon. We found these apartment buildings. They were quite nice, fairly large buildings, and there were several of them. They were spaced maybe a hundred feet apart, something like that. Out behind them, they had little gardens, you know, a little strip of garden for each apartment. And most of them would have a rabbit hutch. They raised their rabbits for meat. And we kicked occupants out of an apartment for our squad, and we went in there. And after we'd been in there a while, one of the guys came up, and he had a funny look on his face and says, "Come with me." And we all went over next door. We got next door, and there was this stink coming out of there, a big stench. And we went in there and our medics were in there. And they had all of these people that were nearly dead, and they were just feeding them a little teaspoon at a time of hot chocolate or something. And if they fed them very much, they'd get sick and die—get sicker and die. And they were just barely alive. And the smell was the smell of death.

And so they told us where it came from—where it came from, and we all got in our truck and we went out there to the camp. On the way saw an older man, made him get on the truck with us to go out there. We didn't bring any of them back. And when we got out there and—I know I didn't see all of it. What I saw was all of these dead people laid outdoors, there on the ground, and it looked like acres of them. And they were—you know, they'd been living in there and—and there was others in there that were—they hadn't brought out. And just a terrible scene. And what we—what we didn't see at all was the underground factories that they had, see. That was back under the Harz Mountains that I told you about. They had these underground tunnels back under the Harz Mountains, and these were slave laborers who were build—who were working on the buzz bombs. And—V-1 rockets, and I think also the V-2s. We saw a lot of V-1s go by and on in. They had a distinctive noise to their engine, you know. And then you'd hear the engine cut off, and you'd know it was going into a dive and everything.

Nordhausen. I've heard since that they called it Dora-Mittelbau or something like that. Dora-Mittelbau, but we just knew it as Nordhausen. The ones that—that could be—had a chance of saving, our medics were working with—on them, and they did just tremendous labor to—to try to save those people and all.

Well, it still bothers me. We went back to our apartment. And the guys in my squad were as fine a young man as they come. Were just—well—nobody was saying a word. It was just almost like they'd forgotten how to talk or something, you know what I mean? They were— It just affected them so much. And the occupant of the apartment came and wanted to get something out of the refrigerator. I don't know, milk for a baby or something, which—you can't imagine anybody saying no. The guy that met them at the door said no and sent them off. It was just kind of beyond words. You know, we'd seen a lot of dead but nothing like that.

[Nothing really prepared you for—]
Nothing.

1

2

3

4

5

6

7

8

9

10

11

13

12

14

15

16

17

18

19

20   21   22

23

TWENTY-SIXTH OFFICER CANDIDATE CLASS
5 July 1943 - 30 October 1943

Company "E" - 4th Platoon

FIRST ROW: Edwards, C.M., Edwards, B.C., Downard, Cronin, Commiskey, Case, Bisceglia.

SECOND ROW: Kelly, Hutchins, Hearne, Hawthorne, Hart, Ham, Goerte, Friedman, Frucht, Freeman.

THIRD ROW: Watson, Tetlow, Sheets, Rice, Lipscomb, Leifheit, Landesman.

25

26

27

28

29

30

31

1. William E. Danner, Jr. (left) with friend

2. George H. Wessels in uniform

3. John Valls in uniform

4. William A. Womack in Paris

5. Raymond S. Watson with friend

6. Herbert U. Stern before the Battle of the Bulge

7. Lee Berg in uniform

8. Chester "Chet" Rohn (right) with his grandfather

9. George H. Wessels

10. Melvin E. Waters (back right) with mother and sister

11. Sigmund Liberman firing 81 mm mortar shells

12. Sigmund Liberman with his squad

13. Ben Love

14. Sigmund Liberman, captured air field in Germany, 1945

15. Raymond S. Watson (right) with friends

16. Herbert U. Stern in North Africa, 1943

17. J. Ted Hartman in uniform

18. Lee Berg (left) at his sister's wedding

19. Sigmund Liberman with mortar in foxhole

20. William E. Danner, Jr.

21. Sigmund Liberman with friend in California.

22. Wilson and Beatrice Canafax

23. Chester "Chet" Rohn (right) with friends

24. Raymond S. Watson (back row, left) and candidate class

25. Ben Love in uniform

26. Melvin Waters in southern Belgium with a Sherman tank

27. Chester "Chet" Rohn in uniform

28. Melvin E. Waters (left) with his friend, "Lefty"

29. Sigmund Liberman at Fordham University

30. Chester "Chet" Rohn, Gmünden, Austria

31. Lee Berg and his dog, Daisy

Photos courtesy of:

Lee Berg Family
Wilson Canafax Family
William Danner Family
Ted Hartman Family
Sigmund Liberman Family
Ben Love Family
Chet Rohn Family
Herb Stern Family
John Valls Family
Melvin Waters Family
Raymond Watson Family
George Wessels Family
William Womack Family

TEXAS VETERAN LIBERATORS HONOR ROLL

The Texas Veteran Liberators Honor Roll catalogs more than three hundred liberators who were stationed in Texas and are known to the Texas Holocaust and Genocide Commission. The list presented here, arranged alphabetically, includes the liberator's name, dates of service, and the name of the camp each person helped liberate. An expanded table is available online. Every effort has been made to provide complete and accurate information. However, we were unable to confirm some ranks and dates of service.

The THGC continues to add names to the Honor Roll. If you participated in the liberation of a Nazi camp or know someone who did, please contact the THGC through its website at http://thgc.texas.gov/.

For the purposes of this project, "Liberator" refers to any serviceperson who was present at any Nazi camp during the first three days of the camp's liberation, or any serviceperson who cared for the survivors and assisted with the removal of the bodies of the victims. The Liberator must have been born in Texas, or lived within the state at some point during their lives.

Salomon Abrego; 1942–1945; Buchenwald

Giles Albriton, Jr.; 1942–1945; Landsberg

Vernon Alexander; Landsberg

John W. Allen; 1945; Dachau

Raymond Allen; 1940–1945; Hurlach

Terry de la Messa Allen; 1913–1948; Dora-Mittelbau

Charles R. Allman; 1942–1945; Dachau

Vincent Amato; 1942–1946; Landsberg

Robert Anderson; 1943–1945; Meitingen Work Camp

Dave Andres; 1943–1945; Ohdruf

Adolfo Anzaldua; 1941–1945; Dachau

Ubaldo Arizmendi; 1941–1945; Dachau

William Ashby ; 1942–1945; Buchenwald

Neal Axelrod; 1942–1964; Dachau

Magdaleno P. Baeza; Dachau

Pedro P. Baeza; 1943–1946; Dachau

Jack Barnes; 1942–1945; Attendorn

Meryl Barnett; 1940–1945; Dachau

Paul K. Barron; Landsberg

Albert Bartschmid, Jr; 1942–1945; Dachau

Rudolf Baum; 1941–1946; Buchenwald

Louis Belsky; 1942–1945; Dora-Mittelbau

William J. Benson; 1942–1945; Landsberg

Lee Berg; 1940–1945; Dachau

Walter I. Berlin; 1941–1967; Nordhausen

Abe Bernstein; 1942–1945; Landsberg

Harry Bernstein; 1941–1945; Risiera di San Sabba

Albert Binko; 1944–1946; Landsberg

J.W. Birdwell; 1944–1946; Dachau

Nathan Birhbaum; Nordhausen

Edward L. Bischoff; 1942–1945; Landsberg

Sidney Blum; 1942–1967; Dachau

Herbert M. Blumenthal; 1942–1945; Dachau

William Bowie; 1943–1946; Dachau

Paul Bowlin; Nordhausen

A. G. Pete Bramble; 1942–1945; Landsberg

Gorman Brewer; 1943–1946; Landsberg

Reuben Brody; Kaufering

Charles Brosseau; 1941–1945; Ohrdruf

Gerard E. Bruson; Gunskirchen

Dale Bryhan; 1942–1945; Landsberg

Ray Buchanan; 1943–1945; Dachau

Werner Busse; 1944–1946; Dachau

Lester R. Calhoun; 1944–1946; Landsberg

Manuel Camarillo; 1942–1945; Buchenwald, Flossenburg

Wilson Canafax; 1942–1946; Buchenwald

Allen B. Canfield; 1942–1945; Landsberg

Walter W. Cardwell; 1943–1945; Dora-Mittelbau

Isaac W. Carey; 1942–1945; Landsberg

Joe C. Carlson; 1941–1945; Nordhausen

Jay Carpenter; 1940–1972; Dachau

Grover Carr; 1944–1945; Dachau

Lillian Carter; 1941–1946 ; Dachau

Henry O. Case; 1942–1945; Landsberg

Loarn Elcaney Carver; 194–1945; Dachau

C. A. Chanet; 1944–1946; Dachau

Kenneth Christopherson; 1943–1945; Dora-Mittelbau

Albert Clauser; Landsberg

Courts Cleveland, Jr; 1942–1945; Hohenwarth POW camps

John R. Cogan; 1943–1945; Ohrdruf

David Cohen; 1941–1945; Ohrdruf, Buchenwald

Lee D. Combs; 1942–1945; Landsberg

Heman R. Cortez; 1940–1945; Spergau

Rupert Costlow; 1942–1952; Landsberg

Anthony H. Couch; 1942–1945; Landsberg

William A. Craig; Nordhausen

Frederick J. Cramer; Buchenwald

Richard Cramer; 1942–1945; Buchenwald

Julien H. Craver; 1942–1945; Landsberg

Arthur W. Crawford; 1942–1945; Landsberg

Robert E. Crawley; 1942–1945; Landsberg

Harry M. Crouse; 1944–1946; Dachau

Grover Cunningham; 1942–1945; Landsberg

James J. Cupples; 1942–1945; Dachau

William "Bill" Danner; 1943–1945; Nordhausen

Thomas D'Aquino; 1943–1946; Dachau

Alfred W. Davis, Jr.; 1942–1946; Dachau

John Dettling Sr.; 1942–1945; Ohrdruf, Buchenwald

Peter DeWetter; 1941–1945; Buchenwald

Myron I. Dickey, Jr.; 1943–1946; Kaufering

Harry Digenthal; 1937–1945; Dachau

William Dippo; 1942–1946; Mauthausen

Douglas Doud; 1942–1945; Dachau

Trenton Dowdle; 1936–1946; Mauthausen, Gusen, Austria

Albert Duncan; 1943–1946; Nordhausen

Robert Dunstan; 1942–1945; Dachau

Hubert L. Dycus; 1942–1945; Landsberg

Robert L. Eaton; 1942–1945; Landsberg

Olav E. Eido; Gunskirchen

Dwight D. Eisenhower; 1941–1945; Ohrdruf

Marie Knowles Ellifritz; 1942–1945; Linz, Mauthausen

Robert Ellis; 1942–1945; Ohrdruf

William Epperson; 1942–1945; Dachau

Joe William Evans; 1941–1945; Ampfing, Schwabigg

Bert Ezell; 1942–1949; Ohrdruf

Julius Feinstein; 1943–1945; Landsberg

Walter J. Fellenz; 1940–1962; Dachau

George X. Ferguson; Dachau

Guillermo Fernandez; Dachau

L.H. Ferris; 1942–1945; Landsberg

John W. Flickinger; Heidelberg

Armando Flores; 1942–1945; Dachau

Thomas C. Foley; 1942–1945; Landsberg

Geronimo Fragua; 1943–1946; Dachau

Ann Franklin; 1944–1946; Dachau

Milford Tipton Fullerton, Jr.; 1942–1947; Salzwedel

Arthur Gaddard; 1942–1945; Dachau

Murray Gaile; Landsberg

Santiago Galaviz; 1942–1945; Nordhausen

Donald K. Garcy; Nordhausen

Glenn R. Gardner; 1941–1945; Dachau

Charles Gentry; 1944–1946; Buchenwald

Nelson A. Geron; 1942–1945; Landsberg

Joe W. Gill; 1940–1946; Itter Castle

Thomas Gillis; 1942–1945; Ohrdruf

Fredrick W. Goldsmith; 1945–1946; DP Transport

Lorenzo B. Gonzalez; 1943–1946; Dachau

Durward B. Gossett; 1942–1945; Dachau

Richard Gottlieb; 1942–1946; Dachau

Raymond E. Gray; 1944–1946; Landsberg

Robert Greenwood; 1942–1945; Dachau

Francis H. Gregg; 1938–1968; Dachau

Wirt T. Grover; 1939–1945; Dachau

Carlos Guzman Guerrer; 1942–1945; Flossenbürg

Lynn H. Guilloud; 1942–1945; Ohrdruf

Jack Gulyas; Mauthausen

Caroll Gustafson; 1943–1947; Dachau

Norm Haley; 1942–1970; Dachau

Clifford L. Hamilton; 1942–1945; Dachau

Samuel M. Harrington; 1943–1946; Dachau

Raymond E. Harris; 1940–;Kaufering

J. Ted Hartman; 1943–1946; Buchenwald, Mauthausen

Birney Havey; 1944–1945; Dachau

A. C. Hays, Jr.; Landsberg

Louis Heidelberger; 1942–1946; Nordhausen

Ramon Herrera; 1942–1945; Maribor

Sydney Hilder; 1943–1945; Dachau

Hence J. Hill; 1944–1946; Buchenwald

Morriss Hoffman; 1943–1945; Dachau

Vernon L. Hosbrook; Mauthausen

Yvonne G. Humphrey; 1942–1945; Dachau

William L. Hunter; 1942–1946; Dachau

Thomas Jimenez; 1944–1946; Gunskirchen

James Melvin Johnson; 1942–1946; Ohrdruf

John P. Jones; 1942–1945; Landsberg

John Paul Jones; 1942–1945; Landsberg

Herman Josephs; 1944–1945; Dachau

Lawrence Jay Kaplan; Buchenwald

Sam Kesner; 1942–1945; Dachau

Oscar L. Kimbell; 1944–1946; Buchenwald

David Klawsky; 1941–1945; Gunskirchen

Walter E. Knapp; 1938–1946; Auschwitz

Audavee B. Knox; 1942–1945; Landsberg

Samuel M. Kogutt; 1943–1946; Flossenbürg

John William Kongable; 1944–1946; Ohrdruf, Buchenwald

Kermit Lee Krueger; 1942–1945; Dachau

Tex Kveton; 1942–1945; Landsberg

Ben Lane; 1942–1945; Mauthausen

Eva LaRae; 1942–1972; Landsberg, Schongau

Henry Larue; 1942–1945; Landsberg

Olan R. Lathrop; Landsberg

Johnny Lawhon; 1944–1945; Dachau, Mauthausen

L.J. Leath; 1944–1946; Dachau

John P. Lee; 1944–1945; Dachau

Joseph V. Lee; 1943–1946; Dachau

Robert Lee; 1942–1945; Landsberg

Jerome Leibs; 1942–1946; Dachau

Walter A. Leigon; 1940–1946; Landsberg

Joe G. Lerma; 1942–1946; Werl

Julian A. Lerner; 1942–1945; Landsberg, Kaufering

Walter J. Levermann; 1943–1946; Dachau

Fred Levy; 1942–1946; Landsberg

Maurice Louis Levy; 1943–1945; Dachau

Eugene B. Lewis; Dachau

Sigmund Liberman; 1943–1945; Nordhausen

Felix Longoria; 1940–1945; Leipzig-Shonsfeld

Jose Angel Lopez; 1941–1946; Buchenwald

Rene Lopez; Kaufering

Ben Love; 1942–1945; Mauthausen

William R. Lynch; 1933–1969; Hurlach

Fred Machol; 1940–1946; Dachau, Volary

Ralph Mackenzie; 1942–1945; Dachau

R. E. Madrey; 1944–1946; Landsberg

Ed Malouf; 1944–1946; Ohrdruf

John Manning; 1941–1962; Landsberg

Stanley Marcus; 1942–1947; Flossenbürg

Isadore A. Margolis; 1943–1945; Weferlingen, Buchenwald

Johnnie Marino; 1941–1945; Hadamar, Kaufering

Ascension "Chon" Martinez; 1942–1945; Ebensee

Ernesto Martinez; 1943–1945; Nordhausen, Sachsenhausen

Ernesto Pedregon Martinez; 1944–1946; Dora-Mittelbau

Calvin Massey; 1943–1945; Landsberg

Henry J. Mattero; 1942–1945; Buchenwald

John L. McConn; 1943–1946; Dachau

Patrick McEnroe, Jr.; Buchenwald

William A. McKenzie; 1942–1945; Buchenwald

Ellen (Richards) McKitrick; 1941–1946; Dachau

Robert McMenamin; 1944–1947; Landsberg

Chester McNamara; Ohrdruf

Guillermo Mendez; 1943–1946; Dachau

Janes D. Menefee; 1941–1945; Landsberg

Zohn Milan; 1944–1946; Landsburg

Gerd Miller; 1942–1946; Dachau, Ebensee, Mauthausen

Jerry Morgan; Dachau

Mary Morris; 1939–; Dachau

Hyatt W. Moser; Hadamar

Arland B. Musser; 1942–1945; Dachau

Quentin F. Naumann; 1943–1946; Dachau

John Nelson; 1941–1945; Ohrdruf

Myers Newman; 1942–1945; Landsberg

James D. Newton; 1940–1945; Langenstan, Buchenwald

Edmundo Nieto; 1942–1945; Landsberg

Robert Osborn; 1943–1946; Dachau

Tom H. Owen; 1943–1946; Dachau

Alfonso Pacheco; Landsberg

Gerald Willard Parker; 1943–1945; Dachau

Alvin Pearson; 1941–1945; Landsberg

Robert Pearson; 1941–1945; Ohrdruf

Albert Pena, Jr.; 1943–1945; Kaufering

Jose M. Perez, Jr; 1942–1945; Landsberg

Charles C. Pervier; 1932–1946; Dachau

Phil Peterson; 1941–1945; Leipzig-Thekla

William Bryant Phelps; 1944–1970; Mauthausen

Thomas Pickens; Buchenwald

Herbert O. Pinno; 1942–1945; Landsberg

Robert H. Pohlman; 1942–1945; Landsberg

Ted Pohrte; Ohrdruf, Mauthausen

John T. Poole; Kaufering

Emilio Portales; 1942–1945; Dachau

David Porter; 1942–1945; Mauthausen

Gerald Powell; 1943–1945; Dora-Mittelbau

Robert Powers; 1941–1945; Landsberg

Lee Price; 1941–1945; Landsberg

Manuel Prieto; Buchenwald

Phillip M. Prieto, M.D.; 1941–1946; Ohdruf, Nordhausen

Alfred M. Proschko; 1943–1946; Dachau

L. W. Puckitt; 1944–1946; Buchenwald

Fred F. Randolph; 1942–1945; Dachau

Joseph S. Ratley; 1942–1945; Landsberg

Francis R. Reese; 1940–1945; Itter Castle

Jesus Jesse Reyes; 1943–1945; Subcamp of Dachau

John Reynolds; 1943–1945; Nordhausen

Harold Richards; 1944–1945; Buchenwald

Everett Riggs; 1941–1945; Landsberg

Salvador Rivera; 1941–1945; Volary

Charles R. Rodgers; 1942–1945; Landsberg

Lawrence R. Rodgers; 1942–1946; Dachau

Rodney Rodgers; 1944–1946; Dachau

Harold Rogers; 1940–1945; Dachau

William E. Rogers; 1941–1946; Dachau

Chester F. Rohn, Jr.; 1943–1945; Mauthausen

Charles Rosenbloom; 1941–1954; Dachau

Albert G. Rosenburg; 1942–1946; Buchenwald

Alice Roth; 1944—; Dachau

Tom Rourke; 1942–1945; Dachau

Gordon Rowe; 1942–1945; Dachau

Felipe T. Roybal; 1942–1945; Wöbbelin

Edwin Rusteberg; 1934–1964; Dachau

Willie Sabrsula; 1942–1945; Gunskirchen

Julien Saks; 1940–1946; Landsberg

Hal Salfen; 1942–1945; Buchenwald

Edward Samuell; 1941–1971; Gunskirchen

George H. Sanger, Jr.; Landsberg

Edmond Sarola; 1942–1945; Landsberg

Alvin Issie Schepps; 1942–1945; Flossenbürg

Albert Schwartz; 1941–1945; Nordhausen

Ira Scott; 1942–1982; Dachau

Jerry Scott; 1941–1947; Dachau

Joseph Sgroi; Dachau

James F. Shafer; 1942–1945; Buchenwald

J. H. Shipp; 1942–1945; Landsberg

Joseph Simpson; 1944–1946; Salzwedel

Jacob Sneiderman; 1940–1945; Wobbelin

Sidney Snyder; Dora-Nordhausen

Edmund Sorola; 1942–1945; Dachau

Felix L. Sparks; 1936–1946; Dachau

Julius Spitzberg; Ebensee

Leonard Staciokas; 1942–1946; Eger

Marvell T. Staggs; Kaufering

Hugh Steffy; 1942–1945; Buchenwald

Cleston Stell; 1944–1946; Buchenwald

Herbert Stern; 1941–1945; Nordhausen

Lawrence R. Stewart; 1941–1945; Dachau

Worth A. Stewart; Landsberg

Sam A. Stockbridge; 1941–1945; Landsberg

Jack W. Sturman; Landsberg

Nathan Swerdlow; 1941–1945; Gusen, Mauthausen

Clayton Miles Taylor; 1934–1960; Ohrdruf

Delbert G. Taylor; 1942–1945; Landsberg

Travis R. Taylor; 1942–1945; Dachau

Reuben George Tepper; Dachau

Donald F. Thompson; Landsberg

Wilbur Eugene "T.D." Thornton; 1942–1945; Dachau

Vernon W. Tott; 1943–1946; Hannover, Ahlem

Angel Trejo; 1944–1946; Dachau

Earl Tweed; 1941–1954; Dinslaken

John Valls; 1943–1945; Bergen-Belsen

Luther Victory; 1942–1945; Mauthausen

George Volkel; 1943–1945; Ohrdruf

Norris Waddill; Eger, Czechoslovakia

William F. Walsh; 1941–1945; Dachau

Clinton Walther; 1944–1946; Wobbelin

Eli Warach; 1941–1945; Mauthausen

Melvin Waters; 1944–1945; Bergen-Belsen

Raymond Watson; 1942–1946; Buchenwald

Harold B. Welch; 1942–1945; Nordhausen

George Wessels; 1944–1946; Wesel Slave Labor

Jack Ellis Westbrook; 1942–1945; Dachau

James White; Kaufering

Curtis R. Whiteway; Hadamar, Dachau

S.J. Willburn; 1941–1945; Buchenwald

Robert William; 1941–1945; Ohrdruf, Zwicka

Harrel W. Williams; 1944–1946; Landsberg

Ted Willner; Bergen-Belsen

George Wise; 1942–1945; Dachau

Leland A. Wittkopp; Bergen-Belsen

Beryl Wolfson; 1941–1945; Dachau

Maurice Wolfson; Salzwedel

William Womack; 1940–1945; Landsberg

Bishop T. Woodson; 1944–1945; Nordhausen, Mittelbau

Thomas C. Yantis; 1943–1962; Dachau

Ed Zebrowski; 1941–1946; Gunskirchen

INDEX

Publication of this book was made possible in part by generous grants from the Texas Holocaust and Genocide Commission and the Friends of the Texas Holocaust and Genocide Commission.